Cahier d'exercices

Voilà!

for the National Framework

2 Clair

JULIE GREEN

Nelson Thornes

Nom:. . . . .

Classe:. . . . .

The author thanks Gwen Berwick and Sydney Thorne, authors of the *Voilà! 2 Clair*
Student's Book on which this Workbook is based.

Published in 2005 by:
Nelson Thornes Ltd
Delta Place
27 Bath Road
CHELTENHAM
GL53 7TH
United Kingdom

07 08 09 / 10 9 8 7 6 5 4 3 2

A catalogue record for this book is available from the British Library

ISBN 978 0 7487 9093 7

Illustrations by Liz Bryan, Stuart Harrison, Simon Girling and Associates
(Mike Lacey), The Organisation (Bernice Lum)

Page make-up by Ken Vail Graphic Design

Printed and bound in Croatia by Zrinski

Miam-miam! J'adore ça!

Pages 26–27 3A

● talk about foods you love and hate ● use regular *-er* verbs

> Moi, je déteste la viande: je suis végétarien. Mais mon frère adore la viande. Ma sœur aime la cuisine indienne. Elle adore aller au restaurant indien. **Julien**

> Alors moi, j'adore le poisson. La cuisine indienne? Ça dépend. Mais mon père adore la cuisine indienne. **Audrey**

> Moi, j'adore le fromage. Mais je n'aime pas l'ail. Berk! Je déteste ça. Ma mère adore l'ail et mon père aussi. **Delphine**

1 a 📖 Look at pictures 1–8. Find someone in the texts above to match each picture.

1 ✓ _Audrey_   5 ✓ _____
2 ✗ _____   6 ✓ _____
3 ✗ _____   7 ✓ _____
4 ? _____   8 ✓ _____

1 b ✏️ Find in three texts, and copy out, a phrase for each picture 1–8.

1 j'adore le poisson _____   _____

_____   _____

_____   _____

2 ✏️ extra! Find in the texts above the French for:

1 I hate _____
2 my sister likes _____
3 she loves _____
4 I love _____
5 I don't like _____
6 my dad loves _____
7 my brother loves _____
8 my mum loves _____

Grammaire: remember the endings for regular *-er* verbs:
je déteste = I hate
tu détestes = you hate
il déteste = he hates
elle déteste = she hates

Photocopying prohibited. *Voilà! 2 Clair Workbook* © Nelson Thornes 2005

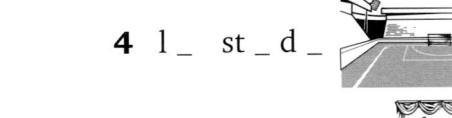

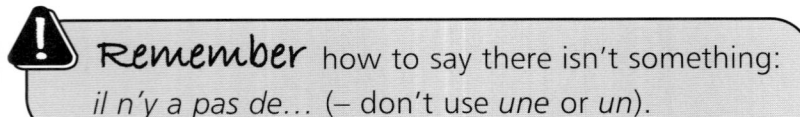

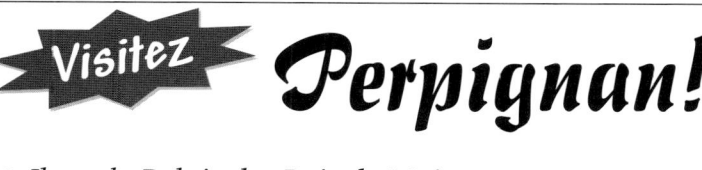

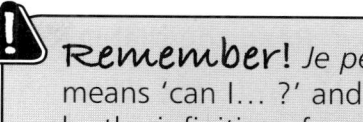

● say what you think of designer clothes ● disagree about clothes – in French

1 a 🗣️ **Read the conversation (with a partner if possible). Be careful with your pronunciation!**

💿 **Listen to it on the CD.**

Clément:	Tu aimes les vêtements de marque, Laura?
Laura:	Oui, j'adore les vêtements de marque. Ils sont de bonne qualité. J'ai des baskets Sketchers.
Clément:	Moi, je n'aime pas les vêtements de marque. Ils sont trop chers.
Lucie:	Oui, c'est du vol. Les vêtements de marque sont ridicules.
Antoine:	Moi, j'aime les vêtements de marque. C'est le top. J'ai un jean Calvin Klein et des baskets Adidas. Ils sont super!

1 b 📖 **Answer the questions.**

1 Who likes designer clothes? _____ _____

2 Who does not like designer clothes? _____ _____

2 ✏️ **Find and copy out the French for:**

1 They are too expensive. _____

2 Designer clothes are ridiculous. _____

3 They are good quality. _____

4 They're the best. _____

5 I like designer clothes. _____

6 I don't like designer clothes. _____

3 ✏️ **extra! Write out three sentences saying what you think about designer clothes. Use sentences from the discussion above.**

_____

_____

_____

Voilà! 2 Clair Workbook © Nelson Thornes 2005

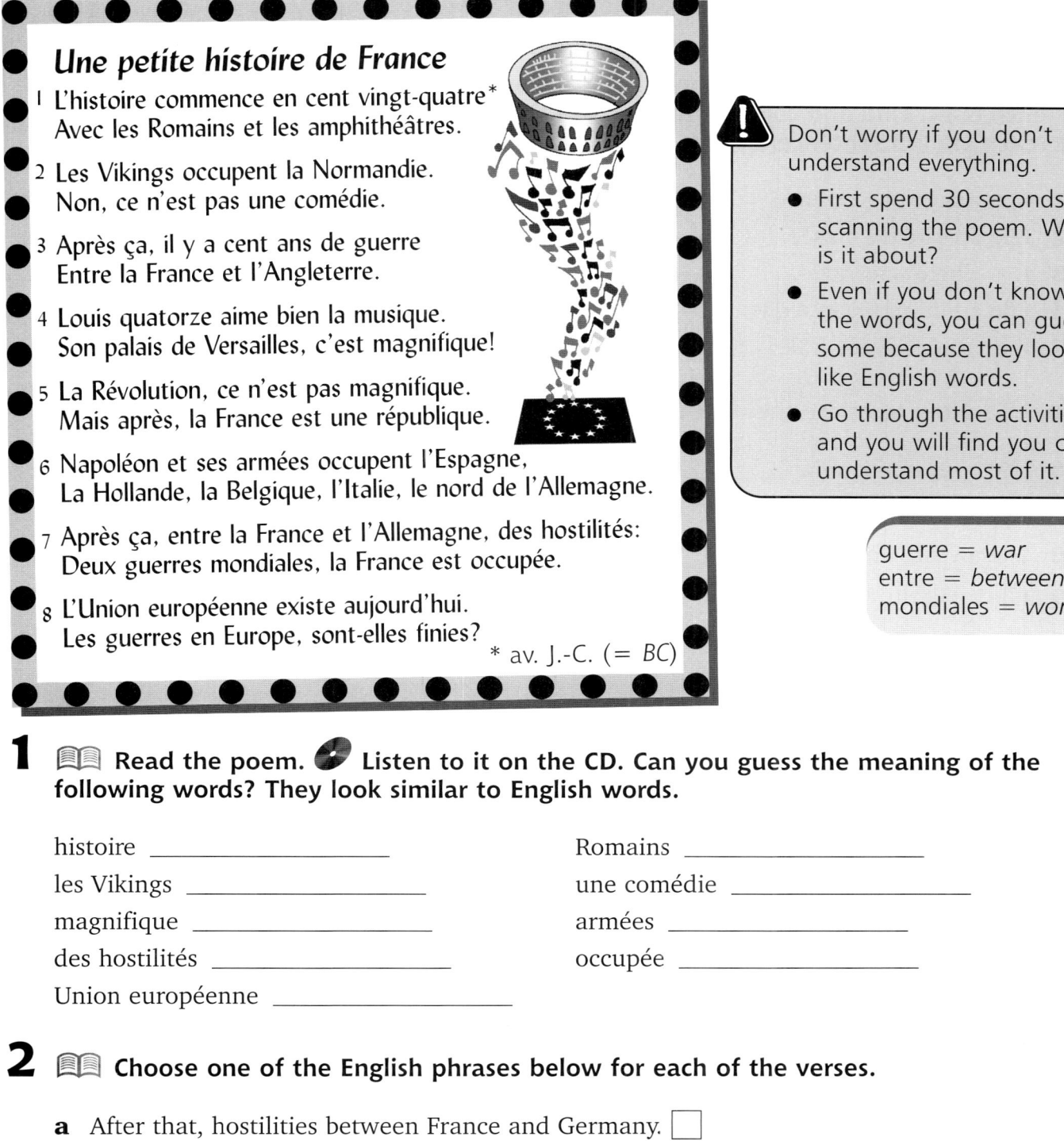

Notes

Voilà! 2 Clair Workbook © Nelson Thornes 2005

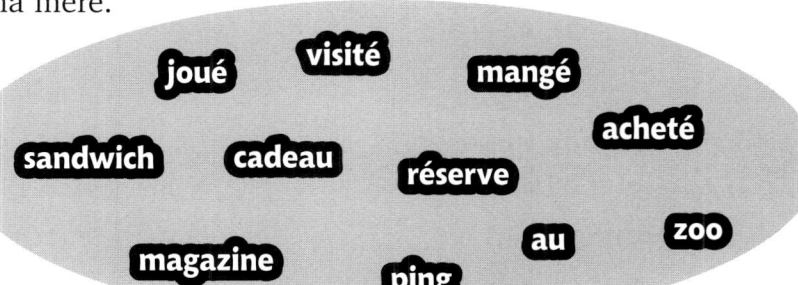

● understand tourist publicity about a town ● write publicity for your town or village

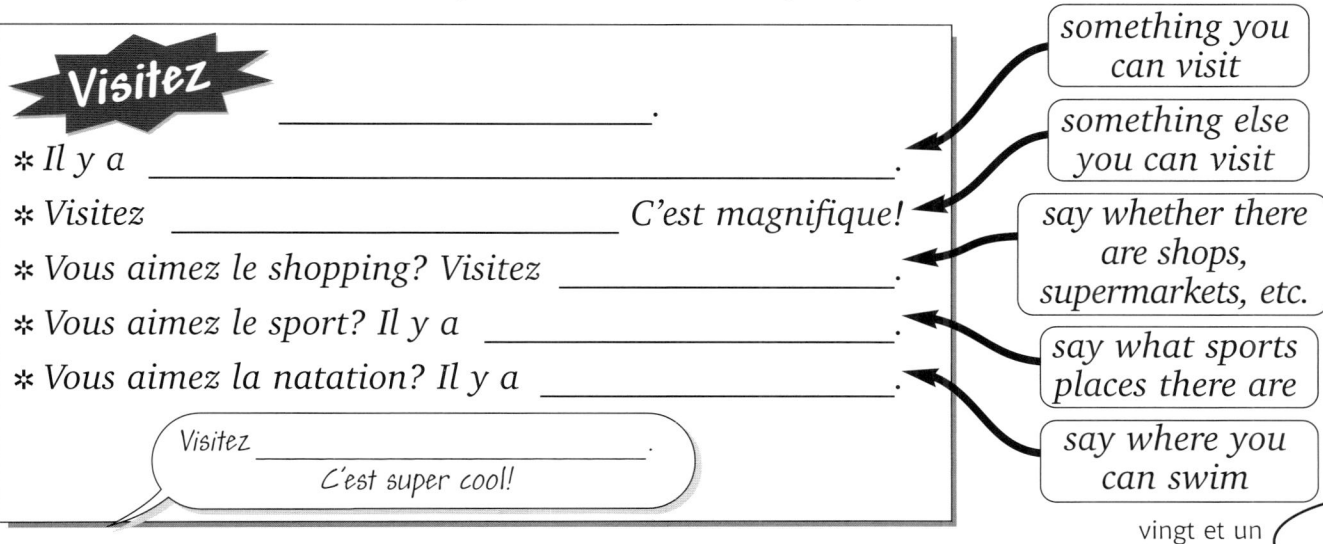

Visitez *Perpignan!*

* Il y a le Palais des Rois de Majorque. C'est un très beau château et il y a de grands jardins aussi.

* Visitez le Castillet, une forteresse. C'est magnifique!

* Vous aimez le shopping? Visitez le centre commercial: il y a des hypermarchés et des magasins.

* Vous aimez le sport? Il y a des centres sportifs, des piscines et des skate parcs.

* Vous aimez la natation? Il y a beaucoup de plages* près de Perpignan.

Visitez Perpignan. C'est super cool!

* plages = beaches

1 📖 **Look at the brochure extract and answer the questions in English.**

1 What is the castle called?

_____

2 What is the name of the fortress?

_____

3 Would Perpignan be good if you like shopping? Why?

_____

4 What is there for people who like sport?

_____

5 Why would it be good for people who like swimming?

_____

⚠ Don't worry if you don't understand every word of the brochure. Read the questions carefully. You should be able to work out the answers from the words you do know.

2 ✏ **Complete the following brochure for an imaginary town.**

Visitez

_____.

* Il y a _____.

* Visitez _____ C'est magnifique!

* Vous aimez le shopping? Visitez _____.

* Vous aimez le sport? Il y a _____.

* Vous aimez la natation? Il y a _____.

Visitez _____. C'est super cool!

something you can visit

something else you can visit

say whether there are shops, supermarkets, etc.

say what sports places there are

say where you can swim

Photocopying prohibited.   *Voilà! 2 Clair Workbook* © Nelson Thornes 2005

● say what the weather is like.

1 a 📖 **Look at the map and sentences 1–10 below. Circle the correct option each time.**

1 Il pleut/fait beau à Paris.
2 Il pleut/fait beau à Calais.
3 Il fait mauvais/fait chaud à St Malo.
4 Il neige/fait chaud à Nice.
5 Il fait beau/neige à Biarritz.
6 Il fait beau/fait mauvais à Perpignan.
7 Il fait beau/pleut à Limoges.
8 Il fait assez chaud/fait mauvais à Bordeaux.
9 Il fait froid/fait beau à Strasbourg.
10 Il neige/pleut à Pau.

(map of France with weather symbols: Calais, St Malo, Paris, Strasbourg, Limoges, Bordeaux, Biarritz, Pau, Perpignan, Nice)

1 b 💬 **Read out the sentences with a partner and check your answers.**

1 c 💿 **Listen to the CD to check.**

2 ✏️ **Write sentences to match the symbols.**

1  St Malo

Il pleut à St Malo.

2 ❄️ Lyon

_____

3  Marseille

_____

4 🥶 Nantes

_____

5 ☀️ Montpellier

_____

6  Calais

_____

7  Biarritz

_____

8  Bordeaux

_____

● suggest activities with *tu veux?* (do you want to?), and respond to other people's suggestions

1 a  Read the dialogue with a partner. Be careful with your pronunciation!

Listen to the CD to check.

1 b 📖 Number the pictures in the order they are mentioned in the dialogue.

A *Tu veux faire du vélo?*

B **Non.**

A *Alors, tu veux aller en ville?*

B **Bof!**

A *Ou alors, tu veux faire du kayak?*

B **Non, c'est barbant!**

A *OK. Tu veux faire du karting?*

B **Non, je n'aime pas ça.**

A *Bon. Alors, tu veux faire une excursion?*

B **Oui, OK.**

A *Super!*

a ☐   **b** ☐   **c** ☐

d ☐   **e** ☐

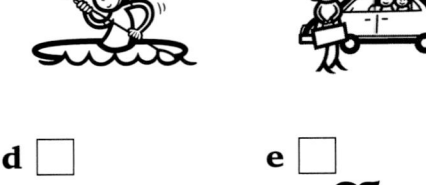

1 c ✏️ Find and copy out:
4 answers indicating you don't want to do something

_____   _____   _____   _____

1 way of agreeing to do something   _____

2 ✏️ Write out a dialogue to match the pictures below. All the language you need is in the dialogue in exercise 1.

A ? → *Tu veux faire du karting?* _____

B ✗ _____

A ? → _____

B ✗ _____

A ? → _____

B ✗ _____

A ? → _____

B ✓ _____

Voilà! 2 Clair Workbook © Nelson Thornes 2005   **Photocopying prohibited.**

• discuss which activities you're going to do

1 ✏️ **Find and cross out the days of the week; then write out the remaining expressions.**

_____

_____

_____

_____

_____

lundifaireduVTTvendredifairedupatinàglacesamedifaired u
théâtremardifairedelavoilejeudifaired u
ev
dimanchefairedelapoterie

2 ✏️ **Read the letter and write the missing expressions into the crossword grid.**

⚠️ Refer to page 47 if you need help with the spellings.

Chère Mamie,

C'est super ici! Demain, je vais

3 → ~~(image)~~ et puis

je vais **5 →** ~~(image)~~

Vendredi, je vais

2 → ~~(image)~~ et le

soir je vais

4 → ~~(image)~~ .

Samedi, je vais

1 → ~~(image)~~ et le

soir, je vais **1 ↓** ~~(image)~~

Bisous

Pauline

3 🗣️💬 **extra!** **Read out the complete letter with a partner. Be careful with your pronunciation!**

💿 **Listen to the CD to check.**

Voilà! 2 Clair Workbook © Nelson Thornes 2005   Photocopying prohibited.

● understand information in a brochure

LE REPTILARIUM DU MONT SAINT-MICHEL

À 4km du Mont Saint-Michel

LA VISITE:
Il y a 200 crocodiles, lézards et serpents. Il y a aussi 300 tortues et des tortues géantes des Seychelles.

INFOS PRATIQUES:
Aire de pique-nique
Boutique avec souvenirs, cartes postales, T-shirts

HORAIRES:

du 1.04 au 30.09	du 1.10 au 31.03
10h–19h	14h–18h

TARIFS:

Adultes:	7,00€
Adolescents (13–18 ans)	6,00€
Enfants (4–12 ans)	5,00€

> ⚠ Don't worry if you don't understand everything. Remember you can sometimes recognise words that look like English words. Often pictures and headings give you clues. Work through the activities and you should be able to understand all the main information.

1 📖 Spend 30 seconds skimming through the information. Can you work out what it is about and pick out three facts? Note them below.

Example: *you can see crocodiles* _____

_____ _____

2 📖 There are four main headings in the brochure. Can you work out what they mean? (The information under each one will give you clues.)

La visite: _____ Horaires: _____

Infos pratiques: _____ Tarifs: _____

3 📖 Now answer the following questions in English.

1 The reptile house is situated near where? _____

2 How much would it cost for one teenager (aged 13) and one adult? _____

3 What are the opening times in November? _____

4 What are the opening times in June? _____

5 Is there a place where you can eat? _____

6 How many tortoises are there? _____

7 Where are the giant tortoises from? _____

8 What could you buy at the shop? _____

Voilà! 2 Clair Workbook © Nelson Thornes 2005

Photocopying prohibited.

● describe a football match ● use the past tense with 'he' and 'she'

1 🔊💬 **Read the text (with a partner if possible). Be careful with your pronunciation!**

💿 **Listen to the CD to check.**

Dimanche dernier, j'ai regardé un match de foot.

C'était Marseille contre Lens. Je suis supporter de Marseille.

C'était un match passionnant et Marseille a gagné 3 à 2.

Marseille a bien joué.

Chapuis a marqué deux buts pour Marseille, et puis Barul a marqué un but pour Lens. Keita a marqué le deuxième but pour Lens.

Puis Marseille a marqué le troisième but et Marseille a gagné.

C'était une victoire pour Marseille!

2 📖 **Find and note:**

the two teams: _____ _____   the final score: _____

a player for Marseille: _____   a player for Lens: _____

3 ✏️ **Find and write the French for:**

1 It was an exciting match. _____

2 Marseille played well. _____

3 I watched a football match. _____

4 Marseille won. _____

5 … scored a goal for Lens. _____

6 It was a victory for Marseille! _____

7 It was Marseille against Lens. _____

8 I am a Marseille supporter. _____

4 ✏️ **extra!** **Write 3–4 sentences about a football match. Use the sentences above and adapt some words.**

⚠️
● You can change the teams, the players and the scores.
● You could say the match was terrible: *C'était une catastrophe*

Voilà! 2 Clair Workbook © Nelson Thornes 2005

● ask for tickets at a museum

1 How many numbers can you find in the wordsnake? Write out the words and then write them out in figures.

vingt-neuf = 29

_____

_____

_____

_____

_____

_____

_____

wordsnake text:
six cinquante - neuf soixante - deux soixante - seize quatre - vingt quatre - trois quatre - vingt trois - neuf vingt - dix-huit - vingt-dix-huit - quatre - vingt-neuf trente trente - deux quarante - trois quarante - huit cinquante - trois quarante

2 a Write out the lines of the dialogue in the right order.

– Trois euros cinquante pour un enfant.
– Merci, monsieur. Au revoir.
– Alors, un adulte et deux enfants. Voilà.
– Bonjour, monsieur. L'entrée, c'est combien, s'il vous plaît?
– C'est sept euros cinquante pour un adulte.
– Et pour un enfant?

_____

_____

_____

_____

_____

2 b Read the dialogue with a partner. Listen to the CD to check.

Voilà! 2 Clair Workbook © Nelson Thornes 2005   Photocopying prohibited.

● say where towns are

1 ✎ Write the directions in the correct place on the diagram.

dans le sud
dans le centre
dans le nord
dans l'est
dans l'ouest

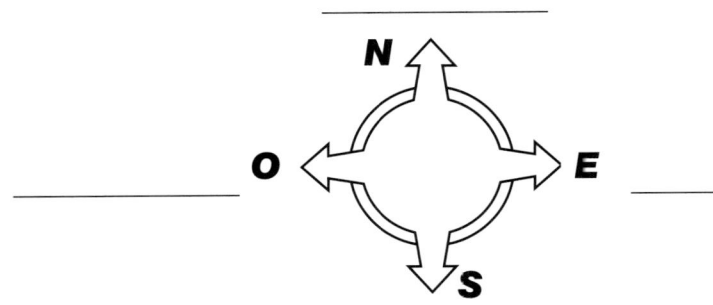

_____

O ⟵   ⟶ E   _____

N

S

_____

2 📖 Look at the map of Belgium. Which towns are being described below?

1 C'est dans l'est de la Belgique.

_____

2 C'est dans le centre de la Belgique.

_____

3 C'est dans le nord de la Belgique.

_____

4 C'est dans le sud de la Belgique.

_____

5 C'est dans l'ouest de la Belgique.

_____

Ostende

Bruxelles

Mons

Verviers

Arlon

3 ✎ *extra!* Look at the map of France. Write six sentences (like 1–5 in exercise 2) for your partner to guess the town.

_____

_____

_____

_____

_____

_____

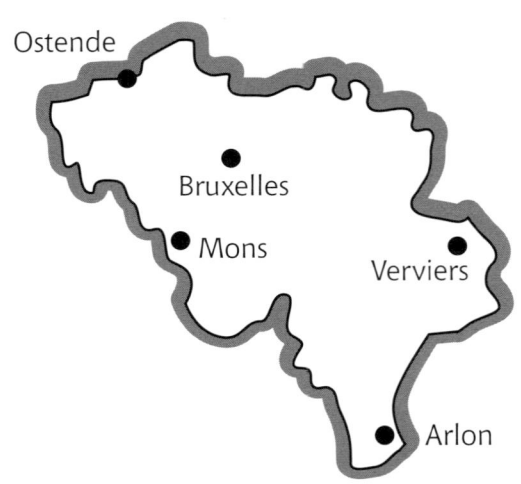

Calais

Strasbourg

Paris

Nantes

Limoges

Lyon

Bordeaux

Marseille

6 ⟩ six

Write the English.

- Remember to use this page to help you learn vocabulary and phrases and to help you with your activities.
- Write the English for the expressions you know. Then look up the ones you don't know on page 15 of the *Voilà! 2 Clair* Student's Book. Write them in too and check your answers.
- Cover up a French column and try to remember the words. Say them out loud. Be careful with your pronunciation!

Un cours d'histoire *A history lesson*

● *say what language is spoken in some countries* ☐

on parle quelle langue? _____

au Pakistan _____

au Sénégal _____

au Brésil _____

en Argentine _____

en Algérie _____

en Inde _____

on parle _____

anglais _____

français _____

espagnol _____

portugais _____

Un cours de géographie *A geography lesson*

● *say some countries and their capitals* ☐

la France _____

la Grande-Bretagne _____

la Belgique _____

l'Allemagne _____

la Suisse _____

la Hollande _____

la capitale de *la France,* c'est *Paris* _____

En classe *In class*

● *use French in class and understand instructions* ☐

un/une élève _____

c'est quoi en français? _____

j'ai fini _____

ça s'écrit comment? _____

pouvez-vous répéter? _____

c'est vrai ou faux? _____

devine! _____

choisis le bon mot pour chaque personne _____

c'est quelle image? _____

trouve et corrige les deux erreurs _____

écris les phrases dans le bon ordre _____

réponds aux questions _____

La France et l'Europe *France and Europe*

● *say where towns are* ☐

c'est où, *Bruxelles*? _____

c'est dans... _____

le nord _____

le sud _____

l'est _____

l'ouest _____

le centre _____

... de *la Belgique* _____

Cross-topic words _____

ou _____ où _____

Voilà! 2 Clair Workbook © Nelson Thornes 2005

Write the English.

- Work in pairs to test each other. Start by one calling out a French phrase for the other to say the English.
- Then say an English phrase and your partner says the French. Swap over. Take care with your pronunciation.
- Note another way that you find useful when you learn vocabulary.

_____

Le sport *Sport*

● *say what sports you played recently* ☐

lundi dernier _____

mardi dernier _____

mercredi dernier _____

jeudi dernier _____

vendredi dernier _____

samedi dernier _____

dimanche dernier _____

j'ai joué… _____

  au foot _____

  au volley _____

  au basket _____

  au ping-pong _____

  au hockey _____

  au badminton _____

  au snooker _____

  au baby-foot _____

  au rugby _____

  au handball _____

Dans le magasin *In the shop*

● *say what you bought* ☐

j'ai acheté… _____

  un CD _____

  un livre _____

  un T-shirt _____

  un magazine sur la musique _____

  un magazine sur l'informatique _____

  un cadeau *pour ma mère* _____

c'était combien? _____

c'était *10 euros* _____

Une visite *A visit*

● *about a visit in the past* ☐

tu as fait quoi le week-end dernier? _____

j'ai visité… _____

  un musée _____

  une réserve naturelle _____

  un zoo _____

  un château _____

c'était bien? _____

oui, c'était… _____

  génial _____

  intéressant _____

non, c'était… _____

  nul _____

  barbant _____

Un e-mail   *An email*

● *talk about a visit* ☐

samedi dernier _____

j'ai mangé… _____

  une glace _____

  un sandwich _____

j'ai joué… _____

  au badminton _____

j'ai visité… _____

  un musée _____

j'ai acheté… _____

  un cadeau _____

c'était… _____

  intéressant _____

cross-topic words

combien? _____   bien _____

Voilà! 2 Clair Workbook © Nelson Thornes 2005   **Photocopying prohibited.**

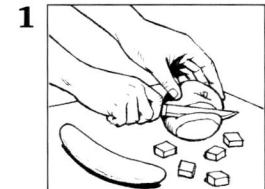

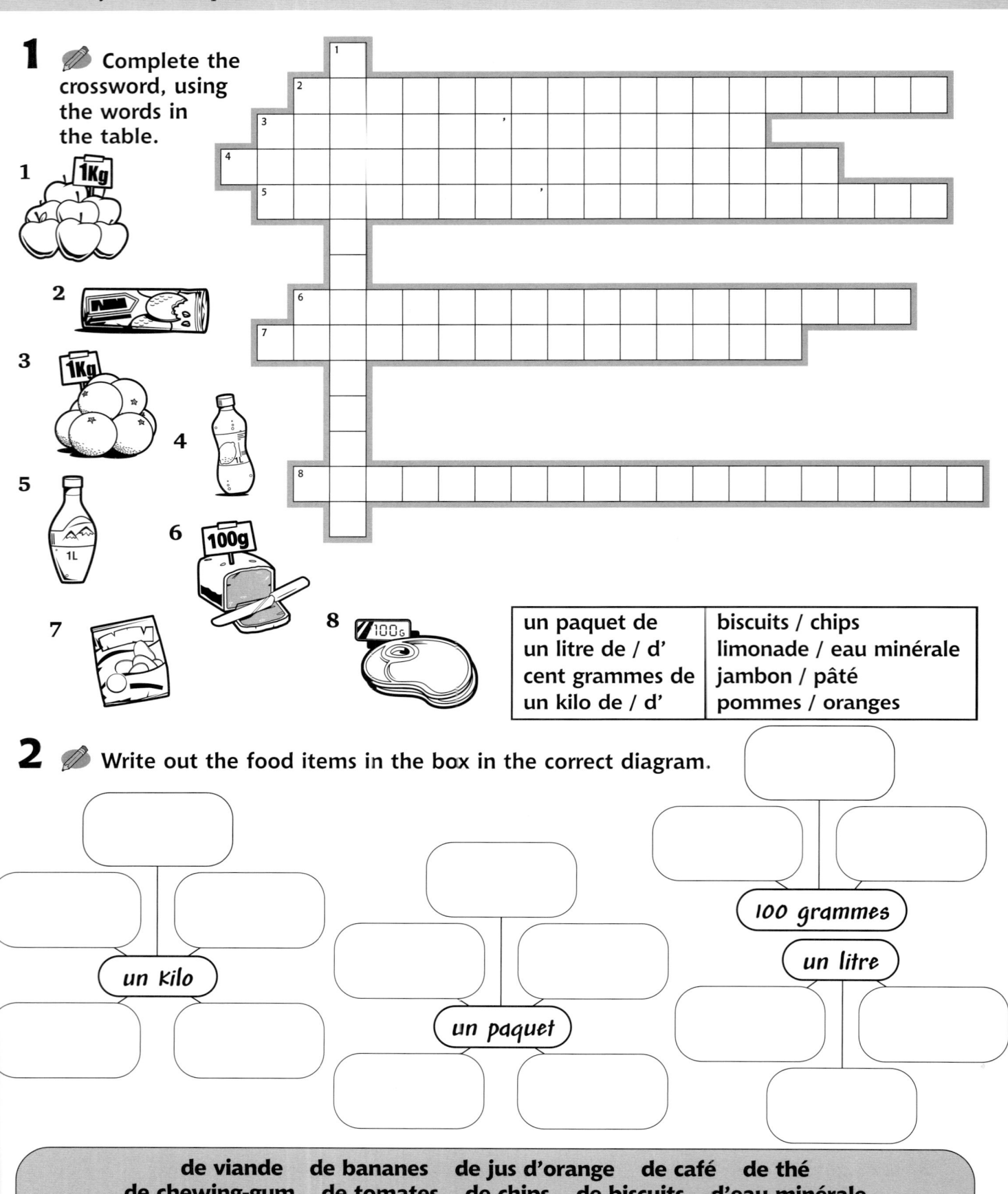

- Remember to use this page to help you learn your new words and phrases.
- Try copying onto a separate piece of paper all the food items on this page under three headings: *j'adore ça, je déteste ça* and *ça dépend*.
  Then write the same lists out from memory. How many did you remember?

Miam! J'adore ça! *Yum! I love that!*

● *talk about foods you love and hate* ☐

j'aime… _____

j'adore… _____

je n'aime pas… _____

tu aimes…? _____

   le fromage _____

   l'ail *m* _____

   le poisson _____

   la viande _____

   la cuisine indienne _____

miam-miam! _____

berk! _____

j'adore ça _____

j'aime ça _____

je n'aime pas ça _____

je déteste ça _____

je ne sais pas _____

ça dépend _____

Un paquet de biscuits *A packet of biscuits*

● *say different quantities of food* ☐

cent grammes de *pâté* _____

cent grammes de *jambon* _____

un kilo de *pommes* _____

un kilo d'*oranges* _____

un paquet de *chips* _____

un paquet de *biscuits* _____

un litre de *limonade* _____

un litre d'*eau minérale* _____

● *buy food and understand prices* ☐

un euro _____

dix centimes _____

vingt _____

trente _____

quarante _____

cinquante _____

soixante _____

soixante-dix _____

soixante-quinze _____

quatre-vingts _____

quatre-vingt-dix _____

quatre-vingt-quinze _____

On fait des courses *Going shopping*

bonjour, madame _____

bonjour, monsieur _____

s'il vous plaît _____

voilà _____

et avec ça? _____

c'est tout? _____

c'est combien? _____

merci _____

au revoir _____

Cross-topic words

merci _____ au revoir _____

dix-sept   **17**

Voilà! 2 Clair Workbook © Nelson Thornes 2005

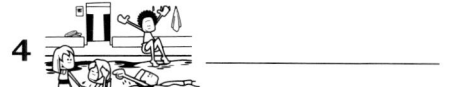

● describe your town or village

> J'habite à Perpignan. C'est une grande ville dans le sud de la
> France près de l'Espagne. J'aime beaucoup ma ville.
> C'est bien pour les touristes: il y a un château et une gare.
> Il y a aussi une belle église, un musée et beaucoup de magasins.
> C'est bien pour les jeunes dans mon quartier: il y a un centre
> sportif, un cinéma, une piscine et un skate parc. C'est genial!
> Sébastien

1 📖 **Read the letter above, then look at the pictures.
Tick the four places that are mentioned.**

a ☐   b ☐   c ☐   d ☐   e ☐   f ☐

2 🖉 **Find and write the French for the following.**

1 It's a big town. _____

2 It's good for young people. _____

3 There's a castle. _____

4 There's also a beautiful church. _____

5 There's a sports centre. _____

6 It's great. _____

7 It's good for tourists. _____

8 near Spain _____

9 I live in… _____

10 I like my town a lot. _____

> ⚠ **Remember** how to say there isn't something:
> *il n'y a pas de…* (– don't use *une* or *un*).

3 🖉 **extra!** **Write out these sentences to say the opposite.**

1 Il y a un centre sportif. **Exemple:** *Il n'y a pas de centre sportif.*
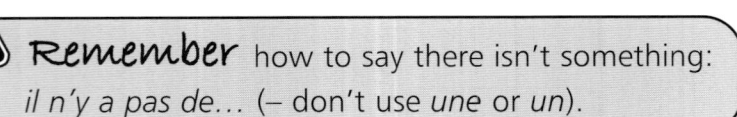

2 Il y a un cinéma. _____

3 Il y a une piscine. _____

4 Il y a un skate parc. _____

5 Il y a un château. _____

Voilà! 2 Clair Workbook © Nelson Thornes 2005   Photocopying prohibited.

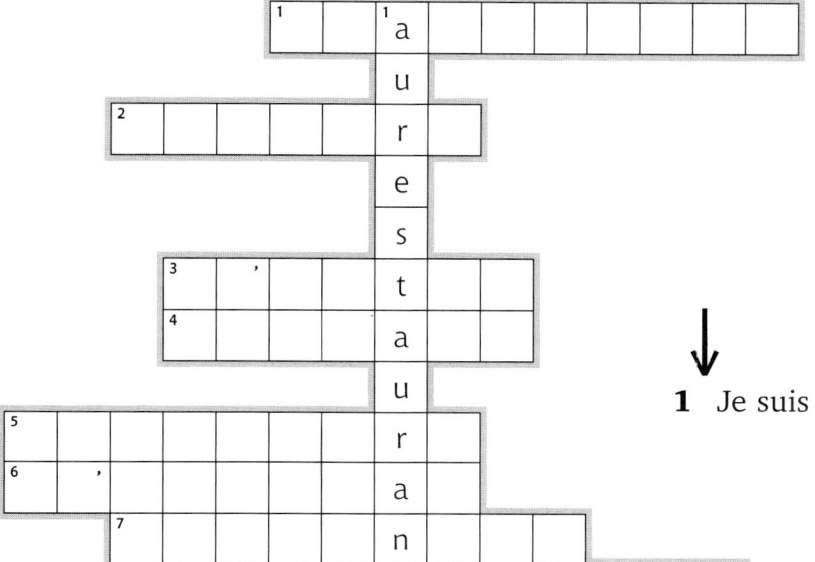

● read about events in French history

Une petite histoire de France

1 L'histoire commence en cent vingt-quatre*
Avec les Romains et les amphithéâtres.

2 Les Vikings occupent la Normandie.
Non, ce n'est pas une comédie.

3 Après ça, il y a cent ans de guerre
Entre la France et l'Angleterre.

4 Louis quatorze aime bien la musique.
Son palais de Versailles, c'est magnifique!

5 La Révolution, ce n'est pas magnifique.
Mais après, la France est une république.

6 Napoléon et ses armées occupent l'Espagne,
La Hollande, la Belgique, l'Italie, le nord de l'Allemagne.

7 Après ça, entre la France et l'Allemagne, des hostilités:
Deux guerres mondiales, la France est occupée.

8 L'Union européenne existe aujourd'hui.
Les guerres en Europe, sont-elles finies?

* av. J.-C. (= BC)

Don't worry if you don't understand everything.
● First spend 30 seconds scanning the poem. What is it about?
● Even if you don't know all the words, you can guess some because they look like English words.
● Go through the activities and you will find you can understand most of it.

guerre = *war*
entre = *between*
mondiales = *world*

1 📖 **Read the poem.** 💿 **Listen to it on the CD. Can you guess the meaning of the following words? They look similar to English words.**

histoire _____   Romains _____

les Vikings _____   une comédie _____

magnifique _____   armées _____

des hostilités _____   occupée _____

Union européenne _____

2 📖 **Choose one of the English phrases below for each of the verses.**

a After that, hostilities between France and Germany. ☐

b The European Union exists today. ☐

c Between France and England. ☐

d Napoleon and his armies occupy Spain. ☐

e With the Romans and the amphitheatres. ☐

f Louis 14th really liked music. ☐

g The revolution was not magnificent. ☐

h The Vikings occupied Normandy. ☐

Voilà! 2 Clair Workbook © Nelson Thornes 2005

Dans le magasin

● past tense: say what you bought

1 🗣️💬 Read the poem out loud with a partner. Be careful with your pronunciation!

💿 Listen to the poem on CD.

> Lundi dernier, j'ai acheté un CD
> J'ai invité Marc et j'ai joué au volley.
>
> J'ai acheté un magazine sur l'informatique
> Et mardi dernier, j'ai écouté de la musique.
>
> J'ai acheté un livre pour mon frère
> Et mercredi dernier, j'ai joué au snooker.
>
> J'ai acheté un T-shirt la semaine dernière
> J'ai aussi acheté un cadeau pour ma mère.
>
> J'ai acheté un cadeau pour Sophie
> Et jeudi dernier, j'ai joué au rugby.
>
> Et puis samedi dernier, c'était fantastique:
> J'ai acheté un magazine sur la musique.

2 ✏️ Find in the poem and write out the words for each picture.

1 _un CD_

2 _____

3 _____

4 _____

5 _____

6 _____

3 ✏️ Find in the poem and write out:

1 verb which means 'I bought' _____

2 words for members of the family _____ _____

3 games _____ _____ _____

4 days of the week _____ _____

_____ _____

Voilà! 2 Clair Workbook © Nelson Thornes 2005

● buy food ● learn a dialogue ● understand instructions in a recipe

1 a ✏ Choose and copy out the correct phrases to complete the dialogue.

– _____

_____

– Voilà. Et avec ça?

– _____

– C'est tout?

– _____

– Quatre euros cinquante.

– _____

Merci. Au revoir.

Un litre d'eau minérale.

Bonjour, madame. Un kilo d'oranges, s'il vous plaît.

Oui, c'est tout. C'est combien?

1 b 💿 Listen to the CD to check.

1 c 💬 extra! Try to learn the dialogue with a partner.

⚠ To learn the dialogue:
● read out the first two lines,
● cover them and say them from memory,
● try the same with the first four lines, then with the first six, and so on.

2 ✏ Write the correct instruction under each picture.

● Lave la pomme et la pêche.
● Pèle l'orange et la banane.
● Coupe la pomme, la pêche, l'orange et la banane en morceaux.
● Mets les fruits dans un grand bol.
● Pèle et coupe un kiwi en morceaux comme décoration.

1

_____

_____

2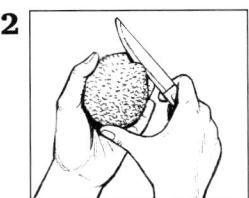

_____

_____

3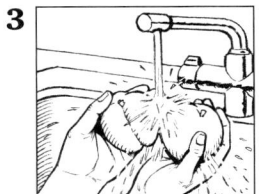

_____

_____

4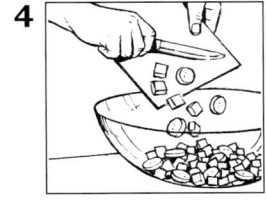

_____

_____

5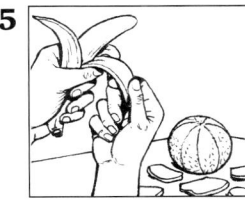

_____

_____

Voilà! 2 Clair Workbook © Nelson Thornes 2005

● tell someone which road to take ● practise a longer sentence

1 Find the words for pictures 1–8.

1 _____

2 _____

3 _____

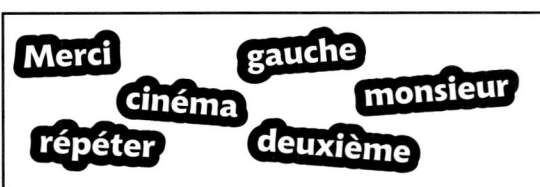
4 _____

5 _____

6 _____

7 _____

8 _____

lecentrecommerciallagarele théâtrelaca thédra lel apis cinelestadelecinémalapatinoire

2 Complete the sentences with a word from the box. Draw a symbol after each one to show what it means.

rue à deuxième gauche la C'est

1 C'est la _____ rue à droite.

2 C'est la première rue à _____

3 _____ la troisième rue à droite.

4 C'est _____ première rue à droite.

5 C'est la troisième rue _____ gauche.

6 C'est la deuxième _____ à gauche.

3 a Complete the dialogue with the missing words.

Merci gauche cinéma monsieur répéter deuxième

– Pardon, _____. C'est où, le _____?

– C'est la _____ rue à gauche.

– Pouvez-vous _____?

– C'est la deuxième rue à _____

– _____, monsieur.

3 b Listen to the CD to check.

3 c extra! Adapt the dialogue to write your own dialogue.

Voilà! 2 Clair Workbook © Nelson Thornes 2005

• Remember to use this page to learn new words and phrases.

• Try writing out the places in two categories: the ones you have where you live, and the ones you don't have.

• Write out a dialogue using as many phrases as you can from this page.

À gauche *On the left*

● *ask the way and give directions* ☐

c'est où… _____

  le stade? _____

  le centre commercial? _____

  le théâtre? _____

  la cathédrale? _____

  la gare? _____

  la place X? _____

c'est à gauche _____

c'est à droite _____

C'est où…? *Where is…?*

● *tell someone which road to take* ☐

pardon, monsieur _____

pardon, madame _____

le cinéma _____

la piscine _____

la patinoire _____

c'est… _____

  la première rue _____

  la deuxième rue _____

  la troisième rue _____

    à gauche _____

    à droite _____

c'est tout droit _____

pouvez-vous répéter? _____

merci _____

au revoir _____

Ma ville/Mon village *My town/village*

● *describe your town or village* ☐

j'habite à… _____

c'est un village _____

c'est une ville _____

près de Bruxelles _____

il y a… _____

et il y a aussi… _____

  un centre sportif _____

  un supermarché _____

  un château _____

  une école _____

  une église _____

mais il n'y a pas de gare _____

Une publicité *An advert*

● *understand tourist publicity about a town* ☐

visitez… _____

  le musée _____

  le parc _____

  la cathédrale _____

il y a… _____

  beaucoup de magasins _____

c'est fantastique _____

c'est intéressant _____

c'est amusant _____

Cross-topic words

près _____ il y a _____

Voilà! 2 Clair Workbook © Nelson Thornes 2005

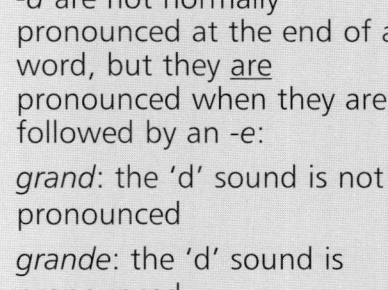

● talk about a day in the past ● use the past tense

1 🖊 Look at the pictures. Find and write out the correct caption for each picture.

💿 Listen to the CD to check.

Le week-end de Danielle

1	2	3

4	5	6

> Puis je suis allée à l'hôpital avec Luc!
> Oh, là, là, ce n'était pas amusant!

> Puis je suis allée au restaurant avec Luc. J'ai mangé du poisson et Luc a mangé un steak.

> Samedi dernier, je suis allée au gymnase.

> Puis je suis allée à la piscine avec Luc. C'était super.

> Dimanche, je suis allée au stade. Luc a joué au foot.

> Le soir, je suis allée à l'hôtel.

2 🖊 **extra!** Write a story of your own. Adapt the one above: change one thing in each sentence.

 Remember how to say 'I went…':
je suis allé… for a male.
je suis allée… for a female.

Voilà! 2 Clair Workbook © Nelson Thornes 2005 **Photocopying prohibited.**

• write and act out a sketch

> Salut, Kévin, tu veux faire du vélo?
> Car aujourd'hui, il fait assez beau.
> Désolé, Nadia, mais je ne peux pas.
> Je dois faire la vaisselle chez moi.
>
> Alors, Kévin, tu veux aller à la patinoire?
> Désolé, Nadia, je dois faire mes devoirs.
> Ou alors, tu veux faire du kayak jeudi?
> Je regrette Nadia, je dois aller chez Ali.
>
> Alors, mardi, tu veux faire une excursion?
> Ou venir chez moi regarder la télévision?
> Non, je dois aller chez mes grands-parents.
> On mange ensemble. C'est un peu barbant!
>
> Alors, ce soir, tu veux venir chez moi?
> Désolé, Nadia, mais je ne peux pas.
> Je dois faire les courses, je dois faire la vaisselle.
> Et puis je dois téléphoner à Danielle... Oh zut!

1 🗣️💬 **Read out the sketch with a partner.**
Be careful, it should rhyme!
💿 **Listen to it on the CD.**

> car = because
> désolé = sorry
> alors = well, then...
> un peu = a little

2 🖊️ **Find and write out the French expression for each picture.**

1 _____

2 _____

3 _____

4 _____

5 _____

6 _____

7 _____

8 _____

3 📖 **extra!** Which of these describe Kévin and which describe Nadia?

patient _____ tactless _____ full of ideas _____ full of excuses _____

● say what you did yesterday ● revise the past tense

> ## La journée de Maxime
>
> Hier c'était lundi. J'ai eu histoire. C'était barbant. À 10 heures,
> j'ai eu anglais. C'était intéressant.
> À midi, j'ai mangé un sandwich au fromage et j'ai bu un jus d'orange.
> Après le collège, je suis allé en ville et j'ai acheté un jean et un
> paquet de chewing-gums.
> Le soir, j'ai regardé la télé. C'était amusant. Puis, j'ai fait mes
> devoirs. C'était barbant!

1 a 📖 Read the text and then number the pictures in the order they are mentioned.

a 　　b 　　c 　　d 　　e 　　f

☐　　　☐　　　☐　　　☐　　　☐　　　☐

1 b 🗣 Read the text out loud. 💿 Listen to the CD to check your pronunciation.

> **Grammaire:** the past tense
> **1a** J'ai _____é is the regular pattern for the past tense:　　**j'ai** *acheté* = I bought
> **1b** Two exceptions:　*j'ai* **eu** = I had　*j'ai* **fait** = I did
> **2**　Use *je suis allé* (boys), or *je suis allée* (girls) to say 'I went'.

2 ✏ Find in the text above and copy out:

7 verbs in the past:

I drank ___*j'ai bu*___

I ate _____

I had _____

I watched _____

I went _____

I did _____

I bought _____

3 opinions: _____

_____　　_____

3 expressions of time:

yesterday _____

after school _____

in the evening _____

Voilà! 2 Clair Workbook © Nelson Thornes 2005　　　　　　Photocopying prohibited.

● discuss which activities you're going to do

1 🖉 **Find and cross out the days of the week; then write out the remaining expressions.**

_____

_____

_____

_____

_____

lundifaireduVTTvendredifairedupatinàglacesamedifaired u
théâtremardifairedelavoilejeudifaired
dimanchefairedelapoterie
que
hev

2 🖉 **Read the letter and write the missing expressions into the crossword grid.**

⚠ Refer to page 47 if you need help with the spellings.

Chère Mamie,

C'est super ici! Demain, je vais

3 → [image] *et puis*

je vais **5 →** [image]

Vendredi, je vais

2 → [image] *et le*

soir je vais

4 → [image] *.*

Samedi, je vais

1 → [image] *et le*

soir, je vais **1 ↓** [image]

Bisous

Pauline

3 🗣 *extra!* **Read out the complete letter with a partner. Be careful with your pronunciation!**

💿 **Listen to the CD to check.**

● practise thinking skills

1 a Find the pairs.

Example: *faire – du cheval*

_____

_____

_____

_____

_____

_____

> faire | ma tante | le matin
> voir un film | j'aime ça
> au centre
> mes cousins | du VTT

> sportif | mes grands-parents
> du cheval | mon oncle
> je n'aime pas ça | du vélo
> au cinéma | à midi

1 b ◯ Compare with your partner and explain your answers.

Examples: *They are opposites; they are places to visit; they're part of one expression.*

2 Work out the logic puzzle. Who is going to do what?

> ⚠️ **Remember!** Each person does only one activity. Once you know who is doing an activity, you can put crosses against all the other activities for that person, and also against the other names for that activity.

- **Clara** va faire de la voile.
- **Marine** va faire du patin à glace. Elle adore ça.
- **Antoine** n'aime pas la poterie, n'aime pas le théâtre et n'aime pas les animaux.
- **Élise** déteste la poterie et n'aime pas les animaux.
- **Louis** n'aime pas la poterie, il n'aime pas le théâtre il n'aime pas faire du VTT. Il aime les animaux.
- **Julien** déteste la voile. Il déteste les sports. Il préfère les activités artistiques.

Antoine						
Clara						
Élise						
Julien						
Louis						
Marine						

Voilà! 2 Clair Workbook © Nelson Thornes 2005

Notes

● say what language is spoken in a country ● use *en* or *au* to mean 'in' a country

1 a ✏️ Find 10 countries in the word snake and write them out.

leBrésillePakistanleSénégall'Argentinel'Indel'Algériel'AustralielaTunisieleMexiqueleMozambique

le Brésil _____   _____

_____   _____

_____   _____

_____   _____

_____   _____

1 b 🗣️ Practise your pronunciation of the countries and check with a partner. Remember how *i* and *é* are pronounced.

💿 Listen to the CD to check.

> **Grammaire:** remember, 'in' a country = *en* or *au*
> ● Many countries are feminine, and use **en**: **en** Algérie, **en** France, **en** Grande-Bretagne
> ● Use **au** with masculine countries: **au** Pakistan

> **Remember!**
> *m* stands for masculine and *f* stands for feminine.

2 a ✏️ Complete the questions with *en* or *au*.

1 On parle quelle langue __en__ France (*f*)?   *On parle français.* _____

2 On parle quelle langue ____ Grande-Bretagne (*f*)? _____

3 On parle quelle langue ____ Sénégal (*m*)? _____

4 On parle quelle langue ____ Pakistan (*m*)? _____

5 On parle quelle langue ____ Brésil (*m*)? _____

6 On parle quelle langue ____ Algérie (*f*)? _____

7 On parle quelle langue ____ Argentine (*f*)? _____

8 On parle quelle langue ____ Inde (*f*)? _____

2 b ✏️ What are the main languages spoken in the countries above (1–8)? Choose and write an answer on the line after each question. Then check with your partner.

On parle français.   On parle arabe et français.   On parle portugais.

On parle espagnol.   On parle urdu, anglais et d'autres langues aussi.

On parle hindi, anglais et d'autres langues aussi.

On parle français et d'autres langues aussi.   On parle anglais.

trois | 3

• say names of countries • say what the capital cities are

1 a ✏ Write the correct country for each car sticker.

1 (**CH**) _la Suisse_   4 (**F**) _____

2 (**NL**) _____   5 (**GB**) _____

3 (**B**) _____   6 (**D**) _____

la Grande-Bretagne

la Suisse

la France   *l'* Allemagne

la Hollande   *la* Belgique

1 b 🗣💬 Practise the pronunciation of each country with your partner. Remember the pronunciation of -*an* and -*gne*.

💿 Listen to the CD to check.

2 ✏ Can you work out what these capital cities are? (If you need help, look at exercise 3.)

1 M _ sc _ _ (Mcsoou)   _Moscou_   6 M _ _ r _ _ (dMiadr)   _____

2 A _ st _ _ d _ _ (madAtsrem) _____   7 B _ _ x _ _ _ _ _ (xeelBurls)   _____

3 _ ar _ _ (sPrai)   _____   8 _ on _ _ _ _ (ersnoLd)   _____

4 B _ _ _ _ (lnreBi)   _____   9 C _ _ _ nh _ _ _ _ (gaueCneop)   _____

5 B _ _ n _ (erenB)   _____   10 _ is _ _ _ _ _ (ebisnoLn)   _____

3 ✏ Match the beginnings and endings to make correct sentences.

💿 Then listen to the CD to check your answers.

1 Berne,   c'est la capitale de la France.

2 Berlin,   c'est la capitale de l'Allemagne.

3 Londres,   c'est la capitale de la Hollande.

4 Bruxelles,   c'est la capitale de la Suisse.

5 Paris,   c'est la capitale de la Grande-Bretagne.

6 Amsterdam,   c'est la capitale de l'Espagne.

7 Moscou,   c'est la capitale du Portugal.

8 Copenhague,   c'est la capitale de la Russie.

9 Lisbonne,   c'est la capitale de la Belgique.

10 Madrid,   c'est la capitale du Danemark.

● speak to the teacher in French ● understand instructions in *Voilà!*

1 🖉 **Find the pairs, reading the clues in the middle to help you. Write out the French.**

1 choose _____ (*four letters are the same in French and English!*)

2 find _____ (*tip: treasure-trove is treasure that has been found!*)

3 reply _____ (*another word for 'reply' is 'respond'*)

4 write _____ (*think of 'scribe' and 'script', replace the 's' with 'é'*)

5 read _____ (*you have to learn this one!*)

6 guess _____ (*a water diviner guesses where there might be water*)

7 correct _____ (*four letters are the same in French and English!*)

8 listen _____ (*think of 'scout out', replace the 's' with 'é', ...*)

9 copy out _____ (*in other words, 're-copy'*)

10 complete _____ (*this one's a doddle!*)

recopie
devine
corrige
écoute
trouve
écris
complète
réponds
lis
choisis

2 🖉 **Match the two halves of sentences, to help you write out the French for sentences 1–7.**

Choisis	quelle image?
C'est	et corrige les deux erreurs.
Trouve	le bon mot pour chaque personne.
Écris	aux questions.
C'est	les phrases dans le bon ordre.
Écoute	vrai ou faux?
Réponds	et répète.

1 Write the sentences in the right order.

_____

2 Choose the correct word for each person.

_____

3 Find and correct the two mistakes.

_____

4 Listen and repeat.

_____

5 Answer the questions.

_____

6 It is true or false?

_____

7 Which picture is it?

_____

3 🖉 **extra!** Unjumble the following sentences. Say what they mean in English.

1 fini! J'ai

_____

2 comment? s'écrit Ça

_____

3 répéter? Pouvez-vous

_____

4 en quoi C'est français?

_____

cinq **5**

● say where towns are

1 ✎ Write the directions in the correct place on the diagram.

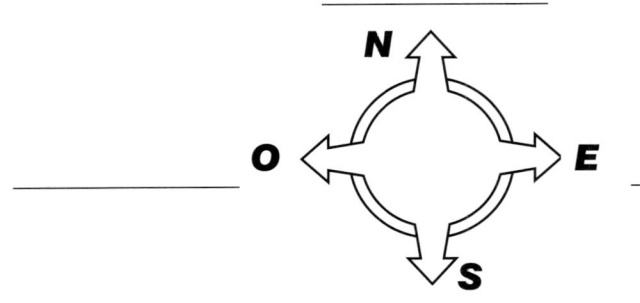

dans le sud
dans le centre
dans le nord
dans l'est
dans l'ouest

2 📖 Look at the map of Belgium. Which towns are being described below?

1 C'est dans l'est de la Belgique.

_____

2 C'est dans le centre de la Belgique.

_____

3 C'est dans le nord de la Belgique.

_____

4 C'est dans le sud de la Belgique.

_____

5 C'est dans l'ouest de la Belgique.

_____

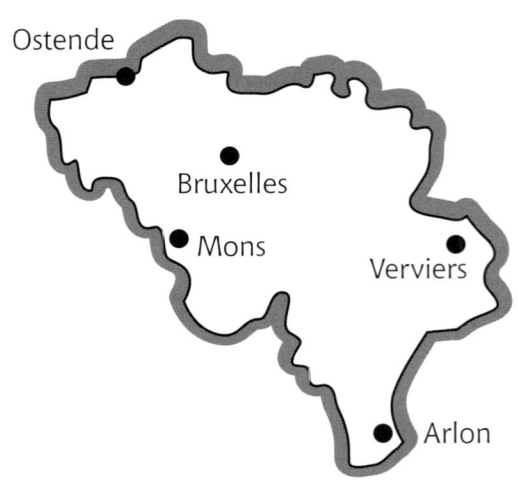

3 ✎ *extra!* Look at the map of France. Write six sentences (like 1–5 in exercise 2) for your partner to guess the town.

_____

_____

_____

_____

_____

_____

Write the English.

- Remember to use this page to help you learn vocabulary and phrases and to help you with your activities.

- Write the English for the expressions you know. Then look up the ones you don't know on page 15 of the *Voilà! 2 Clair* Student's Book. Write them in too and check your answers.

- Cover up a French column and try to remember the words. Say them out loud. Be careful with your pronunciation!

Un cours d'histoire *A history lesson*

- *say what language is spoken in some countries* ☐

on parle quelle langue? _____

au Pakistan _____

au Sénégal _____

au Brésil _____

en Argentine _____

en Algérie _____

en Inde _____

on parle _____

anglais _____

français _____

espagnol _____

portugais _____

Un cours de géographie *A geography lesson*

- *say some countries and their capitals* ☐

la France _____

la Grande-Bretagne _____

la Belgique _____

l'Allemagne _____

la Suisse _____

la Hollande _____

la capitale de *la France*, c'est *Paris* _____

Cross-topic words _____

ou _____ où _____

En classe *In class*

- *use French in class and understand instructions* ☐

un/une élève _____

c'est quoi en français? _____

j'ai fini _____

ça s'écrit comment? _____

pouvez-vous répéter? _____

c'est vrai ou faux? _____

devine! _____

choisis le bon mot pour chaque personne _____

c'est quelle image? _____

trouve et corrige les deux erreurs _____

écris les phrases dans le bon ordre _____

réponds aux questions _____

La France et l'Europe *France and Europe*

- *say where towns are* ☐

c'est où, *Bruxelles*? _____

c'est dans… _____

le nord _____

le sud _____

l'est _____

l'ouest _____

le centre _____

… de *la Belgique* _____

● say what sports you played recently ● compare the present tense and the past tense

1 a 📖 Read sentences 1–10. Tick the ones which are in the past tense.

1 b 🗨 Read sentences 1–10 with your partner. Take care with your pronunciation!

💿 Listen to the CD to check.

> **Grammaire:** *le passé* (the past tense)
> Remember how to form the past tense:
>
> | present | past |
> |---------|------|
> | je joue → ~~je~~'ai jou~~e~~ é → j'**ai** joué |
> | I play | I played |

1 J'ai joué au ping-pong. ☐
2 Je joue au rugby. ☐
3 J'ai joué au baby-foot. ☐
4 Je joue au ping-pong. ☐
5 J'ai joué au volley. ☐

6 Je joue au football. ☐
7 J'ai joué au basket. ☐
8 Je joue au volley. ☐
9 J'ai joué au rugby. ☐
10 J'ai joué au football. ☐

2 🖉 *extra*! Use the table to write a sentence in French for each picture. Then write it in English.

lundi / mardi / mercredi / jeudi / vendredi / samedi / dimanche	... dernier	j'ai joué au	hockey foot ping-pong handball snooker badminton

1 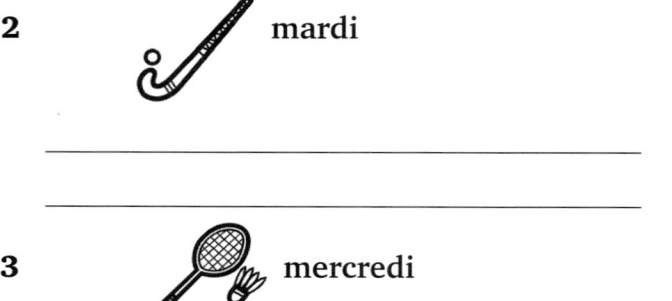 lundi

Lundi dernier, j'ai joué au football.
Last Monday, I played football.

2 mardi
_____
_____

3 mercredi
_____
_____

4  jeudi
_____
_____

5 vendredi
_____
_____

6 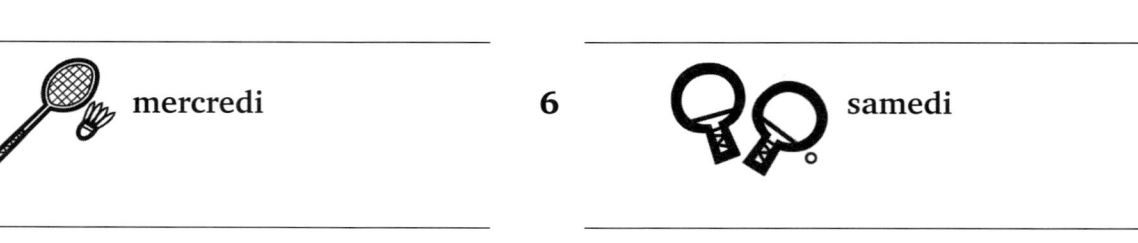 samedi
_____
_____

Voilà! 2 Clair Workbook © Nelson Thornes 2005

● past tense: say what you bought

1 🎤💬 Read the poem out loud with a partner. Be careful with your pronunciation!

💿 Listen to the poem on CD.

> Lundi dernier, j'ai acheté un CD
> J'ai invité Marc et j'ai joué au volley.
>
> J'ai acheté un magazine sur l'informatique
> Et mardi dernier, j'ai écouté de la musique.
>
> J'ai acheté un livre pour mon frère
> Et mercredi dernier, j'ai joué au snooker.
>
> J'ai acheté un T-shirt la semaine dernière
> J'ai aussi acheté un cadeau pour ma mère.
>
> J'ai acheté un cadeau pour Sophie
> Et jeudi dernier, j'ai joué au rugby.
>
> Et puis samedi dernier, c'était fantastique:
> J'ai acheté un magazine sur la musique.

2 ✏️ Find in the poem and write out the words for each picture.

1 _un CD_ _____

2 _____

3 _____

4 _____

5 _____

6 _____

3 ✏️ Find in the poem and write out:

1 verb which means 'I bought' _____

2 words for members of the family _____ _____

3 games _____ _____ _____

4 days of the week _____ _____

_____ _____

neuf **9**

● talk about a visit in the past

1 Find the French for the following opinions:

1 it was brilliant _____

2 it was rubbish _____

3 it was boring _____

4 it was interesting _____

c'étaitintéressantc'étaitnulc'étaitennuyeuxc'étaitgénial

2 Use the table on the right to write a sentence for each picture.

j'ai visité	un château / un zoo / un musée / une réserve naturelle

1 _____ 2 _____ 3 _____ 4 _____

_____

_____

3 Read the note and then adapt it to write your own note. Then try to learn it by heart.

extra! Add another sentence of your own if you can.

Chère **Sarah,**

Lundi dernier, j'ai visité **un château**. C'était **nul!**

À bientôt!

Bisous

Sandrine

● Think what you can change in the note, e.g. the name, the day of the week…

● Use the vocabulary list on page 12 to help you.

_____

_____

_____

_____

_____

_____

_____

_____

● talk about a visit ● use the past tense

1 Complete the following table.

le présent the present tense		le passé the past tense	
French	English	French	English
je visite	I visit	j'ai visité	I _____
je joue	I _____	j'ai joué	I played
je mange	I eat	j'ai mangé	I _____
j'achète	I buy	j'ai acheté	I _____

2 Complete the crossword with the words missing from the sentences. To help you, the missing words are in a box below.

→

2 J'ai visité un _____.

4 J'ai _____ un château.

5 J'ai acheté un _____ sur la musique.

6 J'ai mangé un _____.

8 J'ai _____ un magazine sur l'informatique.

9 J'ai visité une _____ naturelle.

1 J'ai _____ au football.

3 J'ai joué au _____-pong.

5 J'ai _____ une glace.

7 J'ai acheté un _____ pour ma mère.

8 J'ai joué _____ badminton.

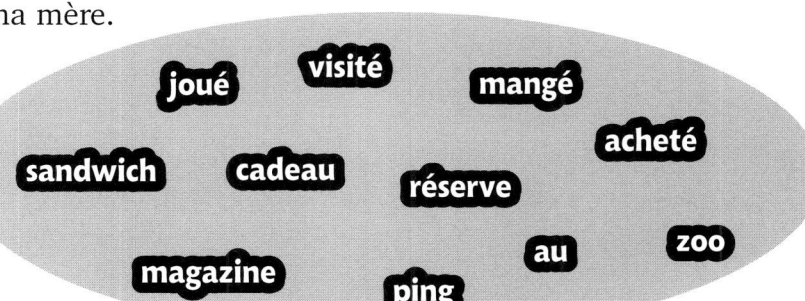

joué   visité   mangé   acheté   sandwich   cadeau   réserve   magazine   ping   au   zoo

Voilà! 2 Clair Workbook © Nelson Thornes 2005

Write the English.

- Work in pairs to test each other. Start by one calling out a French phrase for the other to say the English.
- Then say an English phrase and your partner says the French. Swap over. Take care with your pronunciation.
- Note another way that you find useful when you learn vocabulary.

_____

Le sport *Sport*

● *say what sports you played recently* ☐

lundi dernier _____

mardi dernier _____

mercredi dernier _____

jeudi dernier _____

vendredi dernier _____

samedi dernier _____

dimanche dernier _____

j'ai joué... _____

   au foot _____

   au volley _____

   au basket _____

   au ping-pong _____

   au hockey _____

   au badminton _____

   au snooker _____

   au baby-foot _____

   au rugby _____

   au handball _____

Dans le magasin *In the shop*

● *say what you bought* ☐

j'ai acheté... _____

   un CD _____

   un livre _____

   un T-shirt _____

   un magazine sur la musique _____

   un magazine sur l'informatique _____

   un cadeau *pour ma mère* _____

c'était combien? _____

c'était *10 euros* _____

Une visite *A visit*

● *about a visit in the past* ☐

tu as fait quoi le week-end dernier? _____

j'ai visité... _____

   un musée _____

   une réserve naturelle _____

   un zoo _____

   un château _____

c'était bien? _____

oui, c'était... _____

   génial _____

   intéressant _____

non, c'était... _____

   nul _____

   barbant _____

Un e-mail   *An email*

● *talk about a visit* ☐

samedi dernier _____

j'ai mangé... _____

   une glace _____

   un sandwich _____

j'ai joué... _____

   au badminton _____

j'ai visité... _____

   un musée _____

j'ai acheté... _____

   un cadeau _____

c'était... _____

   intéressant _____

Cross-topic words

_____

combien? _____   bien _____

_____

12 douze

● talk about foods you love and hate ● use regular *-er* verbs

> Moi, je déteste la viande: je suis végétarien. Mais mon frère adore la viande. Ma sœur aime la cuisine indienne. Elle adore aller au restaurant indien. **Julien**

> Alors moi, j'adore le poisson. La cuisine indienne? Ça dépend. Mais mon père adore la cuisine indienne. **Audrey**

> Moi, j'adore le fromage. Mais je n'aime pas l'ail. Berk! Je déteste ça. Ma mère adore l'ail et mon père aussi. **Delphine**

1 a 📖 Look at pictures 1–8. Find someone in the texts above to match each picture.

1 ✓ _Audrey_   5 ✓ _____

2 X _____   6 ✓ _____

3 X _____   7 ✓ _____

4 ? _____   8 ✓ _____

1 b ✏️ Find in three texts, and copy out, a phrase for each picture 1–8.

1 j'adore le poisson _____   _____

_____   _____

_____   _____

_____   _____

2 ✏️ extra! Find in the texts above the French for:

1 I hate _____

2 my sister likes _____

3 she loves _____

4 I love _____

5 I don't like _____

6 my dad loves _____

7 my brother loves _____

8 my mum loves _____

> **Grammaire:** remember the endings for regular -er verbs:
> *je déteste* = I hate
> *tu détestes* = you hate
> *il déteste* = he hates
> *elle déteste* = she hates

treize **13**

● say different quantities of food

1 🖉 Complete the crossword, using the words in the table.

1 [1Kg apples]

2 [chips]

3 [1Kg oranges]

4 [bottle]

5 [1L bottle]

6 [100g]

7 [chewing-gum]

8 [100g pâté]

un paquet de	biscuits / chips
un litre de / d'	limonade / eau minérale
cent grammes de	jambon / pâté
un kilo de / d'	pommes / oranges

2 🖉 Write out the food items in the box in the correct diagram.

un kilo

un paquet

100 grammes

un litre

de viande   de bananes   de jus d'orange   de café   de thé
de chewing-gum   de tomates   de chips   de biscuits   d'eau minérale
de limonade   de jambon   de fromage   de pommes   d'oranges   de pâté

Voilà! 2 Clair Workbook © Nelson Thornes 2005

● buy food　● learn a dialogue　● understand instructions in a recipe

1 a ✎ Choose and copy out the correct phrases to complete the dialogue.

– _____

_____

– Voilà. Et avec ça?

– _____

– C'est tout?

– _____

– Quatre euros cinquante.

– _____

Merci. Au revoir.

Un litre d'eau minérale.

Bonjour, madame. Un kilo d'oranges, s'il vous plaît.

Oui, c'est tout. C'est combien?

1 b 💿 Listen to the CD to check.

1 c 🗩 extra! Try to learn the dialogue with a partner.

⚠ To learn the dialogue:
- read out the first two lines,
- cover them and say them from memory,
- try the same with the first four lines, then with the first six, and so on.

2 ✎ Write the correct instruction under each picture.

- Lave la pomme et la pêche.
- Pèle l'orange et la banane.
- Coupe la pomme, la pêche, l'orange et la banane en morceaux.
- Mets les fruits dans un grand bol.
- Pèle et coupe un kiwi en morceaux comme décoration.

1

_____

_____

2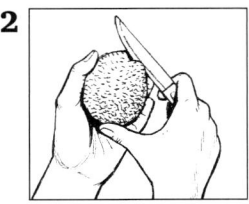

_____

_____

3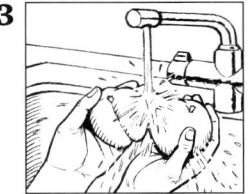

_____

_____

4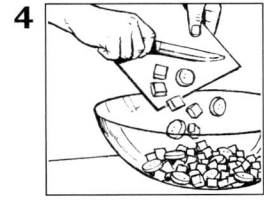

_____

_____

5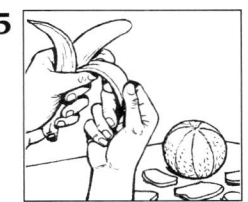

_____

_____

quinze　**15**

● practise thinking skills

1 a  Find the odd-one-out in each set.

1 b 🗩 Compare with a partner and give reasons for your answer.

⚠ **Remember** the following, to help you give reasons for your answers:
● it's masculine
● it's in the past tense
● it has three words, not four
● the rest are things to eat

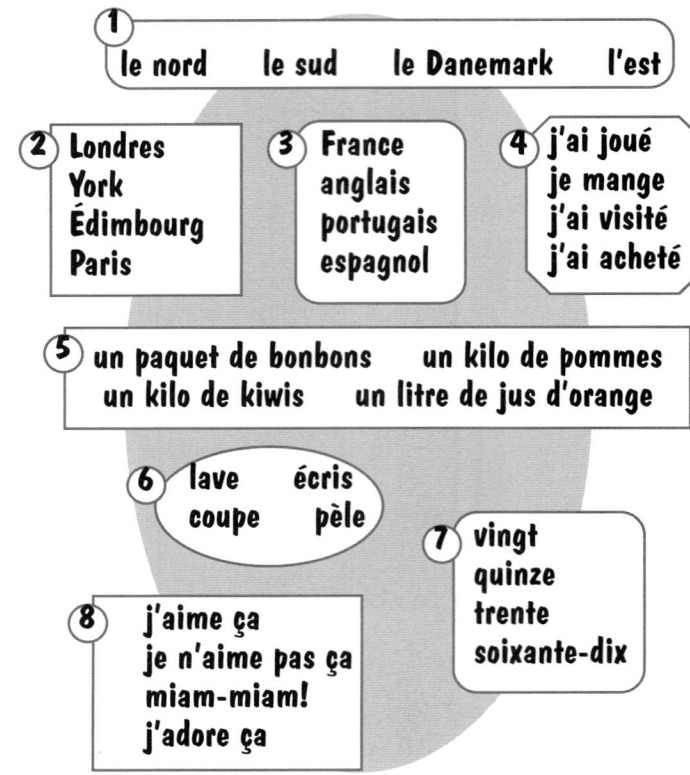

① le nord   le sud   le Danemark   l'est

② Londres / York / Édimbourg / Paris

③ France / anglais / portugais / espagnol

④ j'ai joué / je mange / j'ai visité / j'ai acheté

⑤ un paquet de bonbons   un kilo de pommes / un kilo de kiwis   un litre de jus d'orange

⑥ lave   écris / coupe   pèle

⑦ vingt / quinze / trente / soixante-dix

⑧ j'aime ça / je n'aime pas ça / miam-miam! / j'adore ça

2 ✎ Can you complete the following sequences?

1 lundi, mardi, mercredi, ___*jeudi*___, ___*vendredi*___

2 un euro, trois euros, cinq euros, _____, _____

3 trois, six, neuf, _____, _____

4 vendredi, jeudi, mercredi, _____, _____

5 dix, vingt, trente, _____, _____

6 vingt litres, dix-huit litres, seize litres, _____, _____

7 cinq pêches, dix pêches, quinze pêches, _____, _____

8 dimanche, samedi, vendredi, _____, _____

3 ✎ **extra!** Can you invent some odd-one-out puzzles for your partner to do?

_____

_____

_____

16 seize

• Remember to use this page to help you learn your new words and phrases.

• Try copying onto a separate piece of paper all the food items on this page under three headings: *j'adore ça, je déteste ça* and *ça dépend*.
Then write the same lists out from memory. How many did you remember?

Miam! J'adore ça! *Yum! I love that!*

● *talk about foods you love and hate* ☐

j'aime… _____

j'adore… _____

je n'aime pas… _____

tu aimes…? _____

  le fromage _____

  l'ail *m* _____

  le poisson _____

  la viande _____

  la cuisine indienne _____

miam-miam! _____

berk! _____

j'adore ça _____

j'aime ça _____

je n'aime pas ça _____

je déteste ça _____

je ne sais pas _____

ça dépend _____

Un paquet de biscuits *A packet of biscuits*

● *say different quantities of food* ☐

cent grammes de *pâté* _____

cent grammes de *jambon* _____

un kilo de *pommes* _____

un kilo d'*oranges* _____

un paquet de *chips* _____

un paquet de *biscuits* _____

un litre de *limonade* _____

un litre d'*eau minérale* _____

● *buy food and understand prices* ☐

un euro _____

dix centimes _____

vingt _____

trente _____

quarante _____

cinquante _____

soixante _____

soixante-dix _____

soixante-quinze _____

quatre-vingts _____

quatre-vingt-dix _____

quatre-vingt-quinze _____

On fait des courses *Going shopping*

bonjour, madame _____

bonjour, monsieur _____

s'il vous plaît _____

voilà _____

et avec ça? _____

c'est tout? _____

c'est combien? _____

merci _____

au revoir _____

Cross-topic words merci _____ au revoir _____

dix-sept **17**

● ask the way and give directions ● pronounce *th*

1 ✏ Complete the words with vowels to find six places in a town.

1 l _ c _ th _ dr _ l _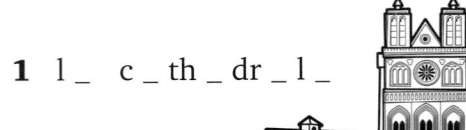

2 l _ g _ r _

3 l _ pl _ c _

4 l _ st _ d _

5 l _ th _ _ tr _

6 l _ c _ ntr _ c _ mm _ rc _ _ l

2 ✏ Choose and copy out a question and an answer from the grid to match symbols 1–6.

C'est où,	le théâtre / la gare / la place Louise / le centre commercial / le stade / la cathédrale	**?**	C'est à gauche. C'est à droite.

1  →

Exemple: *C'est où, la place Louise?*
C'est à droite.

2  →

_____

_____

3 → ←

_____

_____

4  ←

_____

5  →

_____

6  ←

_____

_____

3 🗣💬 Prononciation: *th*

Remember that *th* in French is pronounced like a 't'.

Practise with these words: théâtre, cathédrale, Thomas, thé, menthe, maths

💿 Listen to the CD to check.

4 💬 extra! Read out the questions and answers in exercise 2 with a partner.

Voilà! 2 Clair Workbook © Nelson Thornes 2005

● tell someone which road to take ● practise a longer sentence

1 📖 **Find the words for pictures 1–8.**

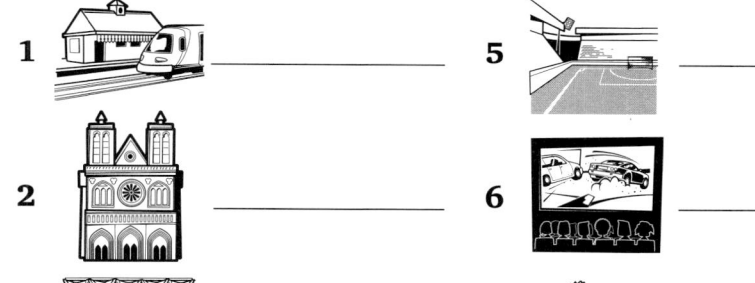

1 _____

5 _____

2 _____

6 _____

3 _____

7 _____

4 _____

8 _____

2 ✏ **Complete the sentences with a word from the box.
Draw a symbol after each one to show what it means.**

rue à deuxième
gauche la C'est

1 C'est la _____ rue à droite.

2 C'est la première rue à _____

3 _____ la troisième rue à droite.

4 C'est _____ première rue à droite.

5 C'est la troisième rue _____ gauche.

6 C'est la deuxième _____ à gauche.

3 a ✏ **Complete the dialogue
with the missing words.**

Merci   gauche
  cinéma   monsieur
répéter   deuxième

– Pardon, _____. C'est où, le _____ ?
– C'est la _____ rue à gauche.
– Pouvez-vous _____ ?
– C'est la deuxième rue à _____
– _____, monsieur.

3 b 💿 **Listen to the CD to check.**

3 c ✏ **extra!** Adapt the dialogue to write your own dialogue.

Voilà! 2 Clair Workbook © Nelson Thornes 2005

● describe your town or village

> J'habite à Perpignan. C'est une grande ville dans le sud de la France près de l'Espagne. J'aime beaucoup ma ville.
> C'est bien pour les touristes: il y a un château et une gare.
> Il y a aussi une belle église, un musée et beaucoup de magasins.
> C'est bien pour les jeunes dans mon quartier: il y a un centre sportif, un cinéma, une piscine et un skate parc. C'est genial!
> Sébastien

1 📖 **Read the letter above, then look at the pictures.**
Tick the four places that are mentioned.

a  b  c  d  e  f

2 🖊 **Find and write the French for the following.**

1 It's a big town. _____

2 It's good for young people. _____

3 There's a castle. _____

4 There's also a beautiful church. _____

5 There's a sports centre. _____

6 It's great. _____

7 It's good for tourists. _____

8 near Spain _____

9 I live in… _____

10 I like my town a lot. _____

 Remember how to say there isn't something:
il n'y a pas de… (– don't use *une* or *un*).

3 🖊 **extra!** **Write out these sentences to say the opposite.**

1 Il y a un centre sportif. **Exemple:** *Il n'y a pas de centre sportif.* _____

2 Il y a un cinéma. _____

3 Il y a une piscine. _____

4 Il y a un skate parc. _____

5 Il y a un château. _____

● understand tourist publicity about a town ● write publicity for your town or village

---

Visitez *Perpignan!*

* Il y a le Palais des Rois de Majorque. C'est un très beau château et il y a de grands jardins aussi.

* Visitez le Castillet, une forteresse. C'est magnifique!

* Vous aimez le shopping? Visitez le centre commercial: il y a des hypermarchés et des magasins.

* Vous aimez le sport? Il y a des centres sportifs, des piscines et des skate parcs.

* Vous aimez la natation? Il y a beaucoup de plages* près de Perpignan.

Visitez Perpignan. C'est super cool!

* plages = beaches

---

1 📖 **Look at the brochure extract and answer the questions in English.**

1 What is the castle called?

_____

2 What is the name of the fortress?

_____

3 Would Perpignan be good if you like shopping? Why?

_____

4 What is there for people who like sport?

_____

5 Why would it be good for people who like swimming?

_____

> ⚠️ Don't worry if you don't understand every word of the brochure. Read the questions carefully. You should be able to work out the answers from the words you do know.

---

2 ✏️ **Complete the following brochure for an imaginary town.**

Visitez

_____ .

* Il y a _____ .   ← something you can visit / something else you can visit

* Visitez _____ C'est magnifique!

* Vous aimez le shopping? Visitez _____ .   ← say whether there are shops, supermarkets, etc.

* Vous aimez le sport? Il y a _____ .   ← say what sports places there are

* Vous aimez la natation? Il y a _____ .   ← say where you can swim

Visitez _____ . C'est super cool!

vingt et un **21**

- Remember to use this page to learn new words and phrases.
- Try writing out the places in two categories: the ones you have where you live, and the ones you don't have.
- Write out a dialogue using as many phrases as you can from this page.

À gauche *On the left*

- *ask the way and give directions* ☐

c'est où… _____

   le stade? _____

   le centre commercial? _____

   le théâtre? _____

   la cathédrale? _____

   la gare? _____

   la place X? _____

c'est à gauche _____

c'est à droite _____

C'est où…? *Where is…?*

- *tell someone which road to take* ☐

pardon, monsieur _____

pardon, madame _____

le cinéma _____

la piscine _____

la patinoire _____

c'est… _____

   la première rue _____

   la deuxième rue _____

   la troisième rue _____

     à gauche _____

     à droite _____

c'est tout droit _____

pouvez-vous répéter? _____

merci _____

au revoir _____

Ma ville/Mon village *My town/village*

- *describe your town or village* ☐

j'habite à… _____

c'est un village _____

c'est une ville _____

près de Bruxelles _____

il y a… _____

et il y a aussi… _____

   un centre sportif _____

   un supermarché _____

   un château _____

   une école _____

   une église _____

mais il n'y a pas de gare _____

Une publicité *An advert*

- *understand tourist publicity about a town* ☐

visitez… _____

   le musée _____

   le parc _____

   la cathédrale _____

il y a… _____

   beaucoup de magasins _____

c'est fantastique _____

c'est intéressant _____

c'est amusant _____

cross-topic words

près _____ il y a _____

● describe friends ● use masculine and feminine adjectives

> J'ai un ami qui s'appelle Daniel. Il aime beaucoup les animaux et les voitures. Il est assez grand et il est amusant. Il est très, très bavard!

> J'ai une amie qui s'appelle Sarah. Elle est assez petite et très sympa. Elle est bavarde aussi. Elle aime beaucoup les ordinateurs et la musique.

> J'ai un ami qui s'appelle Rachid. Il est assez petit et il est très, très sympa. Il aime beaucoup la musique pop et le sport. Il joue au football.

1 a 📖 Read the texts and tick the interests mentioned for each friend.

	🐱🐶	🖥️	🚗	⚽🎾	🎵
Daniel					
Sarah					
Rachid					

1 b ✏️ Find and copy out the French for these phrases.

1 He is funny. _____

2 He is very, very kind. _____

3 She is quite small. _____

4 He is quite small. _____

5 He is very, very chatty. _____

6 She is chatty too. _____

7 He is quite tall. _____

1 c 🗣️ Read out the sentences you have written (with a partner if possible).

💿 Listen to the CD to check.

> ⚠️ **Remember** that -*t* and -*d* are not normally pronounced at the end of a word, but they <u>are</u> pronounced when they are followed by an -*e*:
> *grand*: the 'd' sound is not pronounced
> *grande*: the 'd' sound is pronounced

2 📖 Underline the correct adjectives.

1 Kévin est assez **petit/petite** et très **amusant/amusante**.

2 Sarah est très **grand/grande** et assez **bavard/bavarde**.

3 Ma copine Sandrine est très **petit/petite** et assez **sympa/amusant**.

4 Mon frère est très **grande/grand** et assez **sympa/bavarde**.

> **Remember**, adjectives usually add an -*e* if they are describing someone who is female.
> Exception: *sympa*, which does not change.

vingt-trois **23**

Voilà! 2 Clair Workbook © Nelson Thornes 2005

● talk about your favourite star ● use more masculine and feminine adjectives

1 📖 **Find the French words for the following in the grid.**

1 footballer _footballeur_

2 actress _____

3 male singer _____

4 actor _____

5 female singer _____

6 young _____

7 beautiful _____

8 handsome _____

9 rich _____

10 famous _____

11 American _____

f	o	o	t	b	a	l	l	e	u	r	p
d	u	b	t	m	c	p	a	q	n	i	j
u	l	a	a	c	t	e	u	r	x	c	s
b	e	a	u	x	r	g	s	i	v	h	c
i	a	m	é	r	i	c	a	i	n	e	é
f	e	d	k	g	c	a	i	p	h	g	l
c	h	a	n	t	e	u	r	q	e	k	è
e	y	z	d	w	h	l	o	t	r	q	b
g	q	c	h	a	n	t	e	u	s	e	r
b	e	l	l	e	y	b	j	e	u	n	e

⚠️ Tip: look on page 27 if you have forgotten the French words.

2 📖 **Read the text. On the lines below, write in English the facts given about Kylie in the text.**

She is an actress and...

_____

_____

_____

_____

Ma star préférée, c'est Kylie Minogue. Elle est actrice et chanteuse. Elle est très riche et elle est très célèbre aussi. Elle est australienne.

Elle a joué dans 'Neighbours'. Elle est assez petite et très belle.

3 ✎ **extra!** Complete this paragraph with the words on the right.

Ma _____ préférée, c'est David Beckham. Il est

_____ (English). Il est _____ (rich) et

_____ (famous) aussi. Il est _____ (good looking).

Son _____, c'est le 2 mai.

anglais

beau

anniversaire

star

célèbre

riche

● use *au/à la/aux* to mean 'to the'

Grammaire: remember how to say 'to the...'

au = to the + masculine noun	**au** restaurant, **au** stade, **au** théâtre, **au** gymnase
à la = to the + feminine noun	**à la** gare, **à la** piscine, **à la** patinoire, **à la** cathédrale
à l' = to the + any singular noun (*m* or *f*) beginning with a vowel sound	**à l'**hôtel, **à l'**hôpital

---

1 Complete the crossword with the correct word(s) for 'to the' and the correct place. Use the box above to help you.

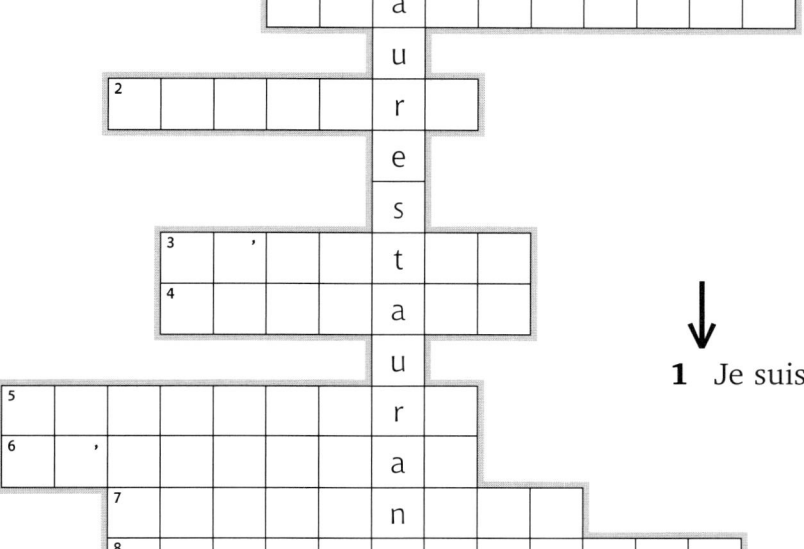

Vertical word: a u r e s t a u r a n t

↓

1 Je suis allé *au* *restaurant*

→

1 Je suis allée _____ _____  **1**

2 Je suis allé _____ _____  **2**

3 Je suis allé _____ _____ **3**

4 Je suis allé _____ _____  **4**

5 Je suis allée _____ _____  **5**

6 Je suis allé _____ _____  **6**

7 Je suis allée _____ _____  **7**

8 Je suis allé _____ _____  **8**

Voilà! 2 Clair Workbook © Nelson Thornes 2005

● talk about a day in the past ● use the past tense

1 🖊 Look at the pictures. Find and write out the correct caption for each picture.

💿 Listen to the CD to check.

Le week-end de Danielle

1	2	3

4	5	6

> Puis je suis allée à l'hôpital avec Luc!
> Oh, là, là, ce n'était pas amusant!

> Puis je suis allée au restaurant avec Luc. J'ai mangé du poisson et Luc a mangé un steak.

> Samedi dernier, je suis allée au gymnase.

> Puis je suis allée à la piscine avec Luc. C'était super.

> Dimanche, je suis allée au stade. Luc a joué au foot.

> Le soir, je suis allée à l'hôtel.

2 🖊 extra! Write a story of your own. Adapt the one above: change one thing in each sentence.

Remember how to say 'I went…':
je suis allé… for a male.
je suis allée… for a female.

• To help you learn the adjectives below, write each one out with the name of someone that matches the adjective. Then try to do it from memory.

• Write down all the places on this page in three columns: the *la* words, the *le* words and those which take *l'*.

• Are there any other ways you find useful to help you learn your vocabulary?

_____

_____

Les copains d'Ali *Ali's friends*

• *describe friends* ☐

j'ai un ami/une amie qui s'appelle... _____

il/elle est... _____

très _____

assez _____

   grand(e) _____

   petit(e) _____

   amusant(e) _____

   bavard(e) _____

   sympa _____

il/elle aime... _____

   les animaux _____

   les ordinateurs _____

   les voitures _____

   le sport _____

   la musique _____

Ma star préférée *My favourite star*

• *talk about your favourite star* ☐

ma star préférée, c'est... _____

il est... _____

   acteur _____

   chanteur _____

   footballeur _____

elle est... _____

   actrice _____

   chanteuse _____

il/elle est... _____

   américain(e) _____

jeune _____

riche _____

célèbre _____

beau _____

belle _____

Les stars et les paparazzi *Stars and the paparazzi*

• *name some places* ☐

le restaurant _____

le gymnase _____

la gare _____

la piscine _____

l'hôpital _____

l'hôtel _____

Tu es une star! *You're a star!*

• *talk about a day in the past* ☐

samedi dernier _____

je suis allé(e)... _____

   au restaurant _____

   au gymnase _____

   à la gare _____

   à la piscine _____

   à l'hôpital *m* _____

   à l'hôtel *m* _____

puis _____

cross-topic words

_____

il _____ elle _____

Voilà! 2 Clair Workbook © Nelson Thornes 2005

● say what the weather is like.

1 a 📖 **Look at the map and sentences 1–10 below. Circle the correct option each time.**

1 Il **pleut/fait beau** à Paris.

2 Il **pleut/fait beau** à Calais.

3 Il **fait mauvais/fait chaud** à St Malo.

4 Il **neige/fait chaud** à Nice.

5 Il **fait beau/neige** à Biarritz.

6 Il **fait beau/fait mauvais** à Perpignan.

7 Il **fait beau/pleut** à Limoges.

8 Il **fait assez chaud/fait mauvais** à Bordeaux.

9 Il **fait froid/fait beau** à Strasbourg.

10 Il **neige/pleut** à Pau.

1 b 💬 **Read out the sentences with a partner and check your answers.**

1 c 💿 **Listen to the CD to check.**

2 ✏️ **Write sentences to match the symbols.**

1  St Malo

Il pleut à St Malo.

2 Lyon

3 Marseille

4 Nantes

5  Montpellier

6  Calais

7  Biarritz

8  Bordeaux

- talk about the weather in different seasons ● give additional, contrasting information
- use negative sentences

> J'habite à Rabat, au Maroc. En été, il fait très chaud et très beau. J'adore l'été. En automne et en hiver, il fait assez beau, mais parfois il pleut et il fait assez froid.
>
> **Leila**

> J'habite à Genève, en Suisse. Au printemps, il fait beau, mais parfois il fait froid. Il fait très beau et chaud en été. En automne, il fait assez froid et il pleut. Mais moi, j'adore l'hiver. Il neige et je fais du ski et du snowboard.
>
> **Laurent**

1 📝 **Read Leila and Laurent's texts, then find the French for the following phrases.**

> ⚠ **Remember** two useful words:
> *très* = very   *assez* = quite

Leila

1 In winter, it's quite nice weather _____

2 I love the summer _____

3 In summer it's very hot _____

4 but sometimes it rains _____

5 It's quite cold _____

Laurent

6 I love winter _____

7 In spring, it's fine _____

8 It's very nice weather _____

9 It snows _____

10 In autumn, it's quite cold _____

2 🗣 **Read the two texts out loud.**

💿 **Listen to the CD to check your pronunciation.**

3 📝 *extra!* **Make these sentences negative.**

1 Il fait chaud. _____

2 Il fait froid. _____

3 Il fait mauvais. _____

4 Il pleut. _____

5 Il neige. _____

6 Il fait beau. _____

> **Grammaire:**
> Remember, use *ne... pas* to make sentences negative.
> *il **ne** pleut **pas*** it doesn't rain, it isn't raining
> *il **ne** fait **pas** beau* we don't have good weather, it's not fine weather

Voilà! 2 Clair Workbook © Nelson Thornes 2005

● say what you do as a family ● adapt useful words from a text

1 a ✏ Find and write out the correct ending for each sentence.

1 b 📖 Draw a small symbol to show what each sentence means.

> **Remember!**
> In these sentences, *on* means 'we'.

1 On invite _____ ☐

2 On va parfois _____ _____ ☐

3 On regarde _____ ☐

4 On discute _____ ☐

5 On _____ _____ ☐

6 On joue _____ ☐

la télé   mange ensemble   mes grands-parents
ensemble   aux cartes   au centre commercial

Vous faites quoi en famille le week-end?

Juliette
Ça dépend. Parfois, le samedi, on va en ville ensemble. Le soir, on mange ensemble. Le dimanche, on regarde la télé ou on invite mes grands-parents.

Le dimanche, on mange ensemble. En été, on joue au tennis ou on joue aux cartes. Le dimanche soir, on discute ensemble ou on écoute de la musique.

Samuel

2 📖 Read the question and the two answers above. **Is it Juliette (J) or Samuel (S)? Who...?**

1 listens to music on Sundays ☐

2 eats with their family on Saturday nights ☐

3 plays tennis ☐

4 discusses things as a family ☐

5 invites grandparents around ☐

6 goes to town with their family ☐

7 watches TV ☐

8 eats with their family on Sundays ☐

9 plays cards ☐

> ● You can change <u>when</u> you did activities: *le dimanche* could become *le lundi*, *le soir* could become *le matin*.
> ● You can change <u>what</u> you did: *on joue au tennis* could become *on joue au football* or *on joue au badminton*.

3 ✏ **extra!** Choose one of the texts above and write it out again, changing at least four details.

● learn about French-speaking communities

La Martinique est dans l'océan Atlantique, au nord de l'Amérique du Sud.
La capitale de la Martinique, c'est Fort-de-France.
Il y a 429 000 habitants.
On parle français et créole.
Le drapeau est le drapeau de la France: bleu, blanc, rouge.
Le climat est tropical. Il fait chaud en été et en hiver. Il pleut en hiver.

La Guyane est en Amérique du Sud, près du Brésil.
La capitale, c'est Cayenne.
Il y a 170 000 habitants.
On parle français et créole.
Le drapeau est le drapeau de la France: bleu, blanc, rouge.
Il fait très chaud en été et en hiver.

1 📖 Read the information on the countries above and complete a form about each of them.

country:		country:	
capital:		capital:	
population:		population:	
languages:		languages:	
flag:		flag:	
climate:		climate:	

2 a 📖 Read the information again and then answer the questions below in French.

La Martinique
1 Quelle est la capitale de la Martinique? _____
2 On parle quelles langues? _____ _____
3 Le drapeau est de quelles couleurs? _____ _____ _____
4 Quel temps fait-il? _____

La Guyane
1 Quelle est la capitale de la Guyane? _____
2 On parle quelles langues? _____ _____
3 Le drapeau est de quelles couleurs? _____ _____ _____
4 Quel temps fait-il? _____

2 b 💬 **extra!** Ask your partner the questions in 2a and check your answers.

Voilà! 2 Clair Workbook © Nelson Thornes 2005

- Work with a partner or someone from your family. Get them to call out the French phrases in the order they come in on the page. Then ask them to call them out in a different order.

- Then get them to say the English, for you to try to remember the French. Make a note of the ones you can't remember and try again another day.

- To help you learn the weather and the seasons, write out the four seasons and the weather matching each one in your country.

Le temps *The weather*

● *say what the weather is like* ☐

quel temps fait-il? _____

il pleut _____

il neige _____

il fait *très* chaud _____

il fait *assez* chaud _____

il fait froid _____

il fait beau _____

il fait mauvais _____

Le climat *The climate*

● *say what the weather is like in different seasons* ☐

en été _____

en automne _____

en hiver _____

au printemps _____

il ne pleut pas _____

il ne fait pas beau _____

En famille *In the family*

● *say what you do as a family* ☐

vous faites quoi
le week-end? _____

on joue *aux cartes* _____

on mange ensemble _____

on discute _____

on regarde la télé _____

on va *au centre
commercial* _____

on invite *mes
grands-parents* _____

Le Québec et le Cameroun   *Quebec and Cameroon*

● *learn about French-speaking countries* ☐

la capitale _____

la population _____

les langues _____

le français _____

l'anglais _____

le climat _____

le drapeau _____

Cross-topic words

quel *m* _____ quelle *f* _____

Voilà! 2 Clair Workbook © Nelson Thornes 2005   **Photocopying prohibited.**

• use *je peux?* (can I?) to ask for permission to do things

1 a ✏️ Choose and copy out the correct ending for each question.

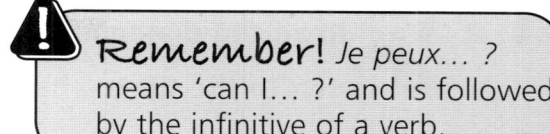

Remember! *Je peux... ?* means 'can I... ?' and is followed by the infinitive of a verb.

1   Je peux ouvrir... _____

2   Je peux fermer... _____

3   Je peux aller... _____

4   Je peux avoir... _____

une feuille de papier?

la fenêtre?

la fenêtre?

aux toilettes?

1 b 💬 Practise the questions until you can say them fluently.
When your partner reads them out, answer with: *Oui, bien sûr* ('Yes, of course') or *Non, tais-toi!* ('No, shut up'). (Say it with expression!)

1 c 📖 Now match the French with the English:

1 Je peux ouvrir... ?   **a** Can I have... ?

2 Je peux fermer... ?   **b** Can I open... ?

3 Je peux aller... ?   **c** Can I go... ?

4 Je peux avoir... ?   **d** Can I close... ?

2 ✏️ *extra!* Choose another ending for each of the phrases.

1   Je peux ouvrir _____?

2   Je peux fermer _____?

3   Je peux aller _____?

4   Je peux avoir _____?

le livre   la porte

cent grammes de jambon

la voiture   des bonbons

à la patinoire

à la piscine

le paquet de biscuits

Voilà! 2 Clair Workbook © Nelson Thornes 2005

● suggest activities with *tu veux?* (do you want to?), and respond to other people's suggestions

1 a 🗣️💬 Read the dialogue with a partner. Be careful with your pronunciation!

💿 Listen to the CD to check.

1 b 📖 Number the pictures in the order they are mentioned in the dialogue.

A *Tu veux faire du vélo?*

B **Non.**

A *Alors, tu veux aller en ville?*

B **Bof!**

A *Ou alors, tu veux faire du kayak?*

B **Non, c'est barbant!**

A *OK. Tu veux faire du karting?*

B **Non, je n'aime pas ça.**

A *Bon. Alors, tu veux faire une excursion?*

B **Oui, OK.**

A *Super!*

a ☐   b ☐   c ☐

d ☐   e ☐

1 c ✏️ Find and copy out:

4 answers indicating you don't want to do something

_____   _____   _____   _____

1 way of agreeing to do something   _____

2 ✏️ Write out a dialogue to match the pictures below. All the language you need is in the dialogue in exercise 1.

A ? → *Tu veux faire du karting?* _____

B ✗ _____

A ? → _____

B ✗ _____

A ? → _____

B ✗ _____

A ? → _____

B ✓ _____

Excuses

● make excuses: say what you have to do ● use the verbs *je peux, tu veux, je dois*

1 a ✎ Fill in the missing vowels to complete the excuses.

1 Je do i s f__r_ l_s c__rs_ s.
2 J_ d__s l_v_r l_ v__t_r_ .
3 J_ d__s f__r_ m_s d_v___rs.
4 J_ d__s f__r_ l_ v__ss_ll_ .
5 J_ d__s _ll_r ch_z m__s gr_nds-p_r_nts.

● Look on page 37 to find help with spelling.
● Remember: *je dois...* means 'I have to...'.

1 b 📖 Match sentences 1–5 above with the pictures.

a  ☐   b  ☐   c  ☐   d ☐   e  ☐

2 📖 Read the two messages and answer the questions below.

Cher Ali,

Je ne peux pas venir à ton barbecue parce que je dois aller chez mes grands-parents. Mais samedi, tu veux faire du vélo?

Amitiés

Sarah

Chère Malika,

Je ne peux pas venir chez toi dimanche parce que je dois aller au restaurant avec ma famille. C'est l'anniversaire de ma mère.

Tu veux venir chez moi samedi après-midi?

Amitiés

Julie

1 What event is Ali having? _____
2 Can Sarah go to it? _____
3 Why? _____
4 What does Sarah invite Ali to do on Saturday? _____
5 On what day was Julie invited to Malika's house? _____
6 What can't she go? _____
7 What is the celebration? _____
8 What does she ask Malika to do on Saturday afternoon? _____

Voilà! 2 Clair Workbook © Nelson Thornes 2005

● write and act out a sketch

Salut, Kévin, tu veux faire du vélo?
Car aujourd'hui, il fait assez beau.
Désolé, Nadia, mais je ne peux pas.
Je dois faire la vaisselle chez moi.

Alors, Kévin, tu veux aller à la patinoire?
Désolé, Nadia, je dois faire mes devoirs.
Ou alors, tu veux faire du kayak jeudi?
Je regrette Nadia, je dois aller chez Ali.

Alors, mardi, tu veux faire une excursion?
Ou venir chez moi regarder la télévision?
Non, je dois aller chez mes grands-parents.
On mange ensemble. C'est un peu barbant!

Alors, ce soir, tu veux venir chez moi?
Désolé, Nadia, mais je ne peux pas.
Je dois faire les courses, je dois faire la vaisselle.
Et puis je dois téléphoner à Danielle... Oh zut!

---

1 🗣️ **Read out the sketch with a partner.**
Be careful, it should rhyme!

💿 **Listen to it on the CD.**

car = because
désolé = sorry
alors = well, then...
un peu = a little

---

2 🖉 **Find and write out the French expression for each picture.**

1 _____

2 _____

3 _____

4 _____

5 _____

6 _____

7 _____

8 _____

---

3 📖 **extra!** **Which of these describe Kévin and which describe Nadia?**

patient _____ *tactless* _____ **full of ideas** _____ *full of excuses* _____

- Use this page to help you learn your vocabulary.
- Highlight any you're not sure of and come back to test yourself on them later.
- Often, writing out the French can help. Try to write a dialogue using as many of the phrases on this page as you can.

En classe *In class*

- *ask permission to do different things* ☐

pardon, madame _____

pardon, monsieur _____

je peux... _____

    ouvrir la fenêtre? _____

    fermer la fenêtre? _____

    aller aux toilettes? _____

    avoir une feuille de papier? _____

oui _____

non _____

bien sûr _____

tais-toi! _____

Suggestions *Suggestions*

- *suggest activities and reply* ☐

tu veux... _____

    faire du vélo? _____

    faire du kayak? _____

    faire du karting? _____

    faire une excursion? _____

    aller en ville? _____

bof... _____

OK _____

alors, tu veux... ? _____

Excuses *Excuses*

- *make excuses* ☐

tu veux venir chez moi? _____

je ne peux pas _____

je dois... _____

    faire mes devoirs _____

    faire la vaisselle _____

    faire les courses _____

    laver la voiture _____

    aller chez mes grands-parents _____

alors, lundi? _____

Un sketch et une lettre *A sketch and a letter*

- *write a thank you letter* ☐

chers Monsieur et Madame *Amrani* _____

merci beaucoup _____

pour *mon* week-end _____

c'était *fantastique*! _____

j'ai beaucoup aimé... _____

amitiés _____

Cross-topic words

bien sûr _____   pardon _____

Voilà! 2 Clair Workbook © Nelson Thornes 2005

● say what you did yesterday ● revise the past tense

La journée de Maxime

Hier c'était lundi. J'ai eu histoire. C'était barbant. À 10 heures, j'ai eu anglais. C'était intéressant.

À midi, j'ai mangé un sandwich au fromage et j'ai bu un jus d'orange. Après le collège, je suis allé en ville et j'ai acheté un jean et un paquet de chewing-gums.

Le soir, j'ai regardé la télé. C'était amusant. Puis, j'ai fait mes devoirs. C'était barbant!

1 a 📖 Read the text and then number the pictures in the order they are mentioned.

a  b  c  d  e  f

☐ ☐ ☐ ☐ ☐ ☐

1 b 🗣 Read the text out loud. 💿 Listen to the CD to check your pronunciation.

Grammaire: the past tense

1a J'ai _____é is the regular pattern for the past tense: **j'ai acheté** = I bought

1b Two exceptions: j'ai **eu** = I had   j'ai **fait** = I did

2 Use je suis allé (boys), or je suis allée (girls) to say 'I went'.

2 ✏ Find in the text above and copy out:

7 verbs in the past:

I drank ___j'ai bu___

I ate _____

I had _____

I watched _____

I went _____

I did _____

I bought _____

3 opinions: _____

_____ _____

3 expressions of time:

yesterday _____

after school _____

in the evening _____

● talk about clothes and colours ● use adjectives

1 **Find 6 items of clothing and 8 colours.**

⚠ Tip: look on page 42 if you have forgotten the French words.

b	l	e	u	b	f	k	q	t	y
p	a	n	t	a	l	o	n	s	e
f	j	z	a	n	h	x	o	h	o
b	t	b	l	a	n	c	i	i	r
s	j	e	a	n	q	d	r	r	a
r	o	u	g	e	v	e	q	t	n
c	e	i	n	t	u	r	e	f	g
e	n	p	c	h	e	m	i	s	e
q	m	a	r	r	o	n	c	a	o
v	e	r	t	j	a	u	n	e	l

2 a Colour the clothes that Tariq and Émilie are wearing.

2 b ✎ **Label the clothes with the name and colour of each item. Read the help box below.**

une chemise blanche

Tariq   **Émilie**

| un T-shirt | un jean | une banane |

| une chemise | un pantalon | une ceinture |

Grammaire: *les adjectifs*

Remember, if the item of clothing is feminine (*une*), you usually add an -*e* on the end of the colour.

If the adjective already ends with an -*e*, don't add anything.

Exceptions!
marron does not change,
blanc becomes *blan**che*** in the feminine.

Use page 42 to check spelling and to see whether an item is masculine or feminine.

Photocopying prohibited.   *Voilà! 2 Clair Workbook* © Nelson Thornes 2005

● say what you think of designer clothes ● disagree about clothes – in French

1 a 🗣️ **Read the conversation (with a partner if possible).**
Be careful with your pronunciation!

💿 **Listen to it on the CD.**

Clément: Tu aimes les vêtements de marque, Laura?
Laura: Oui, j'adore les vêtements de marque. Ils sont de bonne qualité. J'ai des baskets Sketchers.
Clément: Moi, je n'aime pas les vêtements de marque. Ils sont trop chers.
Lucie: Oui, c'est du vol. Les vêtements de marque sont ridicules.
Antoine: Moi, j'aime les vêtements de marque. C'est le top. J'ai un jean Calvin Klein et des baskets Adidas. Ils sont super!

1 b 📖 **Answer the questions.**

1 Who likes designer clothes? _____ _____

2 Who does not like designer clothes? _____ _____

2 🖊️ **Find and copy out the French for:**

1 They are too expensive. _____

2 Designer clothes are ridiculous. _____

3 They are good quality. _____

4 They're the best. _____

5 I like designer clothes. _____

6 I don't like designer clothes. _____

3 🖊️ **extra!** **Write out three sentences saying what you think about designer clothes.**
Use sentences from the discussion above.

_____

_____

_____

● give your opinion about different clothes ● use adjectives in the plural

1 a 🖉 **Separate the words to write out the sentences.**

1 Tuaimeslescravates? _____

2 Tuaimesleschemisesblanches? _____

3 Tuaimeslesjeansnoirs? _____

4 TuaimeslesT-shirtslarges? _____

5 Tuaimeslespullslarges? _____

6 Bof,çadépend. _____

7 Ouij'aimelespullslarges. _____

8 Nonjen'aimepaslesjeansnoirs. _____

1 b 🗣 **Ask your partner questions 1–5 above. They should reply *Oui*, *Non* or *Bof, ça depend*.**

2 🖉 **Answer the following questions, in full sentences.**

⚠ Remember: plural adjectives add an -*s*.

1 Tu aimes les ceintures rouges?
Oui, j'aime les ceintures rouges./Non, je n'aime pas les ceintures rouges.

2 Tu aimes les jeans larges?

_____

3 Tu aimes les pulls oranges?

_____

4 Tu aimes les pantalons jaunes?

_____

5 Tu aimes les cravates noires et blanches?

_____

3 🖉 **extra! Can you make up three more sentences with the clothing items and different colours or adjectives? Check your spellings on page 42.**

_____

_____

Voilà! 2 Clair Workbook © Nelson Thornes 2005

• To help you remember your past tense verbs, write a sentence with each of the verbs listed below. Add an opinion to each sentence.

• To help you remember clothes, write the words for the clothes in order of preference, then add your opinion next to each one.

• Are there any other ways you find useful to help you learn your vocabulary?

_____

Hier *Yesterday*

● *say what you did yesterday* ☐

hier _____

après le collège _____

le soir _____

j'ai eu... _____

   maths _____

   anglais _____

   français _____

   histoire _____

   dessin _____

   sciences _____

j'ai acheté... _____

   un magazine _____

   un T-shirt _____

j'ai regardé... _____

   la télé _____

j'ai fait... _____

   mes devoirs _____

● *say what it was like* ☐

c'était... _____

   amusant _____

   intéressant _____

   barbant _____

Un T-shirt orange *An orange T-shirt*

● *talk about clothes and colours* ☐

un pantalon _____

un jean _____

un T-shirt _____

une chemise _____

une banane _____

une ceinture _____

rouge _____

jaune _____

orange _____

bleu(e) _____

vert(e) _____

noir(e) _____

blanc *m*, blanche *f* _____

marron *m/f* _____

Un débat *A debate*

● *say what you think of designer clothes* ☐

tu aimes les vêtements de marque? _____

pourquoi? _____

j'aime _____

je n'aime pas _____

ils sont trop chers _____

ils sont de bonne qualité _____

c'est le top! _____

c'est du vol! _____

Tu aimes ça? *Do you like that?*

● *give your opinion about clothes* ☐

tu aimes... ? _____

j'aime... _____

je n'aime pas... _____

   les jeans noirs *m* _____

   les chemises blanches *f* _____

   les pulls larges *m* _____

   les cravates *f* _____

bof, ça dépend _____

Cross-topic words

trop _____   pourquoi? _____

Voilà! 2 Clair Workbook © Nelson Thornes 2005

● say what you are going to do

1 🖉 Complete the diagram using the words below.

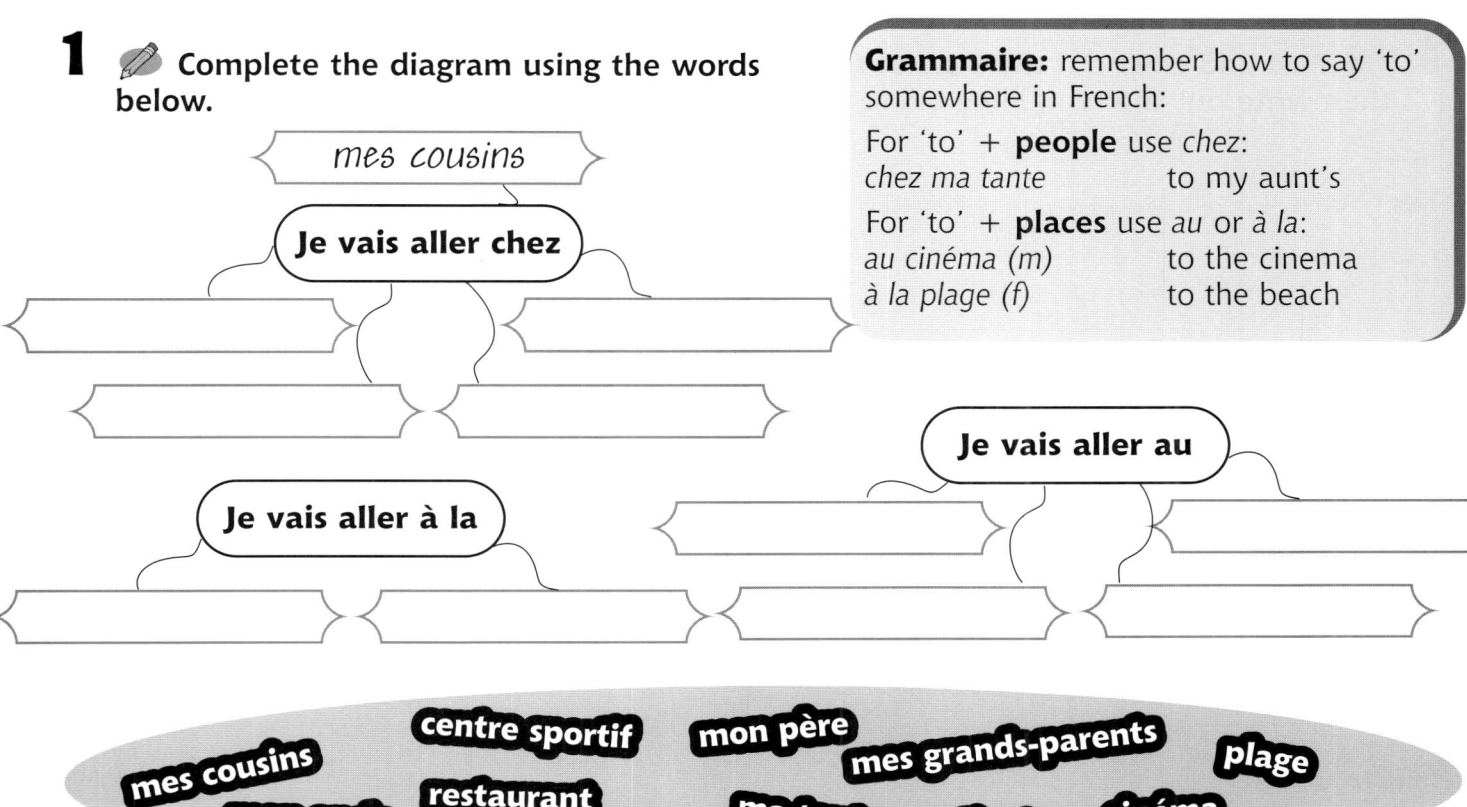

> **Grammaire:** remember how to say 'to' somewhere in French:
>
> For 'to' + **people** use *chez*:
> *chez ma tante*   to my aunt's
>
> For 'to' + **places** use *au* or *à la*:
> *au cinéma (m)*   to the cinema
> *à la plage (f)*   to the beach

mes cousins

Je vais aller chez

Je vais aller au

Je vais aller à la

mes cousins   centre sportif   mon père   mes grands-parents   plage
mon oncle   restaurant   bowling   ma tante   patinoire   cinéma

2 🖉 Look at the symbols below and write a sentence for each day, using the expressions from the diagram in exercise 1.

lundi

mardi

mercredi

jeudi

vendredi   père

samedi   cousins

dimanche

Lundi, je vais aller au cinéma.

Voilà! 2 Clair Workbook © Nelson Thornes 2005

● discuss which activities you're going to do

1 🖉 **Find and cross out the days of the week; then write out the remaining expressions.**

_____

_____

_____

_____

_____

_____

lundifaireduVTTvendredifairedupatinàglacesamedifaired
théâtremardifairedelapeinturejeudifaireduc
dimanchefairedelapoterie

2 🖉 **Read the letter and write the missing expressions into the crossword grid.**

⚠ Refer to page 47 if you need help with the spellings.

Chère Mamie,

C'est super ici! Demain, je vais

3 → _____ et puis

je vais **5 →** _____

Vendredi, je vais

2 → _____ et le

soir je vais

4 → _____ .

Samedi, je vais

1 → _____ et le

soir, je vais **1 ↓** _____

Bisous

Pauline

3 🗣 **extra!** Read out the complete letter with a partner. Be careful with your pronunciation!

💿 Listen to the CD to check.

● describe a planned school trip

Excursion à Disneyland Resort Paris

- On va partir à 7h30.
- On va arriver à 9h30.
- Le matin, on va visiter Discoveryland.
- À midi et demi, nous allons manger dans le café Hyperion.
- Puis, on va voir le spectacle Videopolis.
- On va rentrer au collège à 21h00.

1 📖 **Read the text above and then complete the plans below in English.**

Plans for the trip to _____

We're going to _____ at 7.30am.

We're going to _____ at 9.30.

_____ we're going to visit Discoveryland.

At _____ we're _____ to eat in the Hyperion café.

Then we're _____ the show 'Videopolis'.

We're _____ to school at 9pm.

2 ✏️ **extra!** **Write some plans in French for a trip to the town of Blois.**

trip to Blois
leave: 8.00   arrive: 10.00
morning: visit le château de Blois
lunch: eat in a restaurant
afternoon: see a film at the cinema
return: 9.30pm

_____

_____

_____

_____

_____

_____

Stratégies! Think of the trip as six steps:
1 leaving
2 arriving at destination
3 morning activity
4 lunch
5 afternoon activity
6 return
Write a sentence for each step. Use the text in exercise 1 to help you.

Voilà! 2 Clair Workbook © Nelson Thornes 2005

● practise thinking skills

1 a Find the pairs.

Example: *faire – du cheval*

_____

_____

_____

_____

_____

_____

faire · ma tante · le matin · voir un film · j'aime ça · au centre · mes cousins · du VTT

sportif · mes grands-parents · du cheval · mon oncle · je n'aime pas ça · du vélo · au cinéma · à midi

1 b ⌒ Compare with your partner and explain your answers.

Examples: *They are opposites; they are places to visit; they're part of one expression.*

2 Work out the logic puzzle. Who is going to do what?

⚠ **Remember!** Each person does only one activity. Once you know who is doing an activity, you can put crosses against all the other activities for that person, and also against the other names for that activity.

- **Clara** va faire de la voile.
- **Marine** va faire du patin à glace. Elle adore ça.
- **Antoine** n'aime pas la poterie, n'aime pas le théâtre et n'aime pas les animaux.
- **Élise** déteste la poterie et n'aime pas les animaux.
- **Louis** n'aime pas la poterie, il n'aime pas le théâtre il n'aime pas faire du VTT. Il aime les animaux.
- **Julien** déteste la voile. Il déteste les sports. Il préfère les activités artistiques.

Antoine						
Clara						
Élise						
Julien						
Louis						
Marine						

- Ask your partner or a family member to test you. Ask them to call out the English for you to say the French, first in the order they are listed here, and then in a different order.

- Highlight the ones you get wrong and test yourself again later.

- To help you learn all the different activities below, write out the days of the week and, by each one, two activities you'd like to do.

Le week-end *The weekend*

- *say what you're going to do* ☐

demain _____

ce week-end _____

lundi _____

mardi _____

mercredi _____

jeudi _____

vendredi _____

samedi _____

dimanche _____

je vais aller... _____

    au centre sportif _____

    au cinéma _____

    au bowling _____

    à la plage _____

    chez ma tante _____

    chez mon oncle _____

    chez mon père _____

    chez mes grands-parents _____

Au centre d'activités *At the activity centre*

- *discuss which activities you're going to do* ☐

tu vas faire quoi demain? _____

je vais faire... _____

    du cheval _____

    du VTT _____

    du patin à glace _____

du théâtre _____

de la voile _____

de la poterie _____

j'aime ça _____

c'est amusant _____

c'est génial _____

je n'aime pas ça _____

c'est difficile _____

Planète Futuroscope *Planet Futuroscope*

- *describe a planned school trip* ☐

à 7h30 _____

le matin _____

à midi _____

puis _____

on va partir _____

on va arriver _____

on va rentrer _____

on va... _____

    manger dans un café _____

    voir un film _____

    voir un spectacle _____

Cross-topic words

_____

demain _____ chez _____

_____

Voilà! 2 Clair Workbook © Nelson Thornes 2005

● understand information in a brochure

LE REPTILARIUM DU MONT SAINT-MICHEL

À 4km du Mont Saint-Michel

LA VISITE:
Il y a 200 crocodiles, lézards et serpents. Il y a aussi 300 tortues et des tortues géantes des Seychelles.

INFOS PRATIQUES:
Aire de pique-nique
Boutique avec souvenirs, cartes postales, T-shirts

HORAIRES:

du 1.04 au 30.09	du 1.10 au 31.03
10h–19h	14h–18h

TARIFS:

Adultes:	7,00€
Adolescents (13–18 ans)	6,00€
Enfants (4–12 ans)	5,00€

> ⚠ Don't worry if you don't understand everything. Remember you can sometimes recognise words that look like English words. Often pictures and headings give you clues. Work through the activities and you should be able to understand all the main information.

1 📖 **Spend 30 seconds skimming through the information. Can you work out what it is about and pick out three facts? Note them below.**

Example: *you can see crocodiles* _____

_____   _____

2 📖 **There are four main headings in the brochure. Can you work out what they mean? (The information under each one will give you clues.)**

La visite: _____   Horaires: _____

Infos pratiques: _____   Tarifs: _____

3 📖 **Now answer the following questions in English.**

1 The reptile house is situated near where? _____

2 How much would it cost for one teenager (aged 13) and one adult? _____

3 What are the opening times in November? _____

4 What are the opening times in June? _____

5 Is there a place where you can eat? _____

6 How many tortoises are there? _____

7 Where are the giant tortoises from? _____

8 What could you buy at the shop? _____

● describe a football match ● use the past tense with 'he' and 'she'

1 🎤💬 **Read the text (with a partner if possible). Be careful with your pronunciation!**
💿 **Listen to the CD to check.**

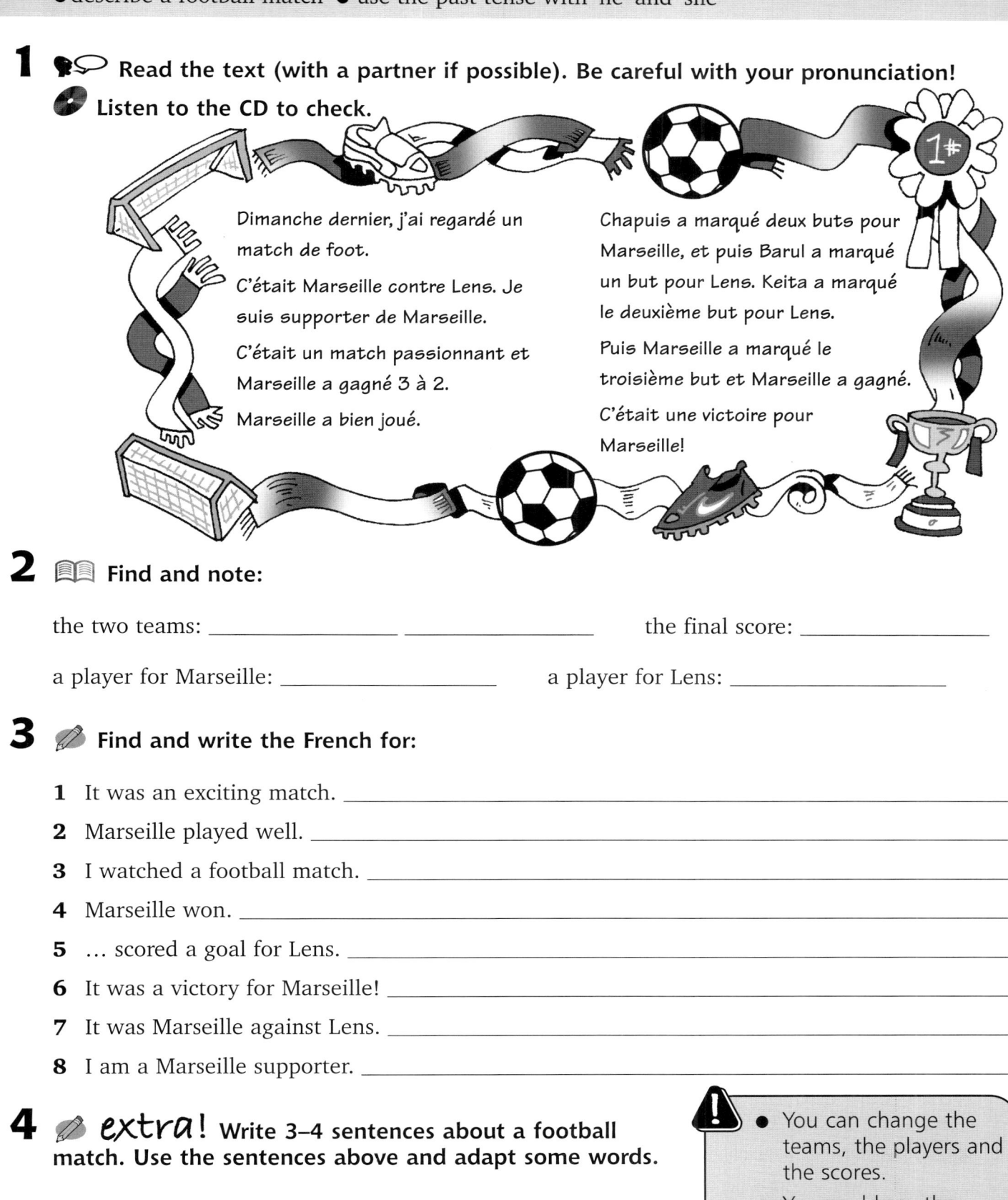

Dimanche dernier, j'ai regardé un match de foot.

C'était Marseille contre Lens. Je suis supporter de Marseille.

C'était un match passionnant et Marseille a gagné 3 à 2.

Marseille a bien joué.

Chapuis a marqué deux buts pour Marseille, et puis Barul a marqué un but pour Lens. Keita a marqué le deuxième but pour Lens.

Puis Marseille a marqué le troisième but et Marseille a gagné.

C'était une victoire pour Marseille!

2 📖 **Find and note:**

the two teams: _____ _____ the final score: _____

a player for Marseille: _____ a player for Lens: _____

3 ✏️ **Find and write the French for:**

1 It was an exciting match. _____

2 Marseille played well. _____

3 I watched a football match. _____

4 Marseille won. _____

5 ... scored a goal for Lens. _____

6 It was a victory for Marseille! _____

7 It was Marseille against Lens. _____

8 I am a Marseille supporter. _____

4 ✏️ ***extra!*** **Write 3–4 sentences about a football match. Use the sentences above and adapt some words.**

⚠️
● You can change the teams, the players and the scores.
● You could say the match was terrible: *C'était une catastrophe*

quarante-neuf **49**

● describe a visit to a friend ● say what 'we' did

Grammaire: the past tense
● Use *on a...* to say what 'we' did: *on a mangé* we ate   *on a bu* we drank

1 For each picture, choose and copy out the correct sentence from the box below.

1	2	3

4	5	6

a **Le soir, on a commandé une pizza.**   **Puis, on a bavardé.** b

c **Hier, je suis allé chez un copain.**   **D'abord, on a regardé un match de foot à la télé.** d

e **Après ça, on a bu un coca.**   **Puis, on a lu des magazines et des BD.** f

2 Find and copy out the matching time expressions in French.

then → _____   after that → _____   first of all → _____

in the evening → _____   yesterday → _____

3 *extra!* Try to change one thing in each of the six sentences in exercise 1.
Write them out. The ideas below might help you.

Remember you can change various things:
● the person who did the action: *on a lu* → *j'ai lu*
● the nouns: *on a bu un coca* → *on a bu un café*
● the time marker: *Hier* → *Le week-end dernier*

chez ma tante
une limonade
le week-end
on a joué aux cartes
un match de tennis
j'ai lu

Voilà! 2 Clair Workbook © Nelson Thornes 2005

Photocopying prohibited.

● ask for the right bus ● give instructions

1 🖉 Separate out the words and write out the dialogue.

- _____
  _____
- _____
- _____
  _____
- _____
- _____
- _____

(scrambled text around the box:) Pardonmonsieure'estquelbuspourlecinéma?Prenezle19.Pardonjen'aipascompris.Pouvez-vousrépéter?Prenezlebusnuméro19.Merci,monsieur.Deux.Pren

2 🗫 Read the dialogue with a partner. Be careful with your pronunciation!

💿 Listen to the CD to check.

3 🖉 Write a dialogue for the following situations.

⚠ To write your dialogues, use the one in exercise 1 as a model. You will need to change the place you're going to, the bus number, and *monsieur* to *madame* if you're speaking to a woman.

1 You ask a woman which bus it is to the swimming pool; it's number 23.

_____
_____
_____
_____
_____
_____

2 You ask a man which bus it is to the skating rink; it's number 54.

_____
_____
_____
_____
_____
_____
_____

Voilà! 2 Clair Workbook © Nelson Thornes 2005

- To help you learn the vocabulary, read the French out loud, being very careful and very precise with your pronunciation. Say each word three times, trying to sound as French as possible.

- Record yourself and listen back: do you sound French? If not, try again!

Le parc safari *The safari park*

- *use the past tense to describe a visit* ☐

hier _____

j'ai visité _____

   un parc safari _____

j'ai vu... _____

   des girafes _____

   des autruches _____

   des rhinocéros _____

   des éléphants _____

   des hippopotames _____

   des zèbres _____

c'était *bien* _____

c'était *génial* _____

j'ai mangé... _____

   un hamburger _____

   des frites _____

j'ai bu... _____

   un coca _____

   une limonade _____

Le match de foot *The football match*

- *describe a football match* ☐

samedi dernier _____

j'ai regardé... _____

   un match de foot _____

à la télé _____

c'était *X* contre *Y* _____

X a bien joué _____

X a marqué un but _____

X a gagné *3 à 0* _____

c'était... _____

   un match passionnant _____

   une catastrophe _____

Chez mon copain *At my friend's house*

- *describe a visit to a friend* ☐

hier _____

puis _____

après ça _____

le soir _____

je suis allé(e)... _____

   chez un copain/
   une copine _____

on a bavardé _____

on a vu un match
   de foot à la télé _____

on a bu *un coca* _____

on a lu des magazines
   et des BD _____

on a commandé
   une pizza _____

Le bus pour le stade *The bus to the stadium*

- *ask for the right bus* ☐

pardon, monsieur/madame _____

c'est quel bus pour *le stade*? _____

prenez le *16* _____

merci, monsieur/madame _____

de rien _____

cross-topic words

hier _____ le soir _____

● suggest what food to take on a picnic ● say what you eat and drink

1 🖊 Complete the crossword. All the phrases are in the box below.

➡

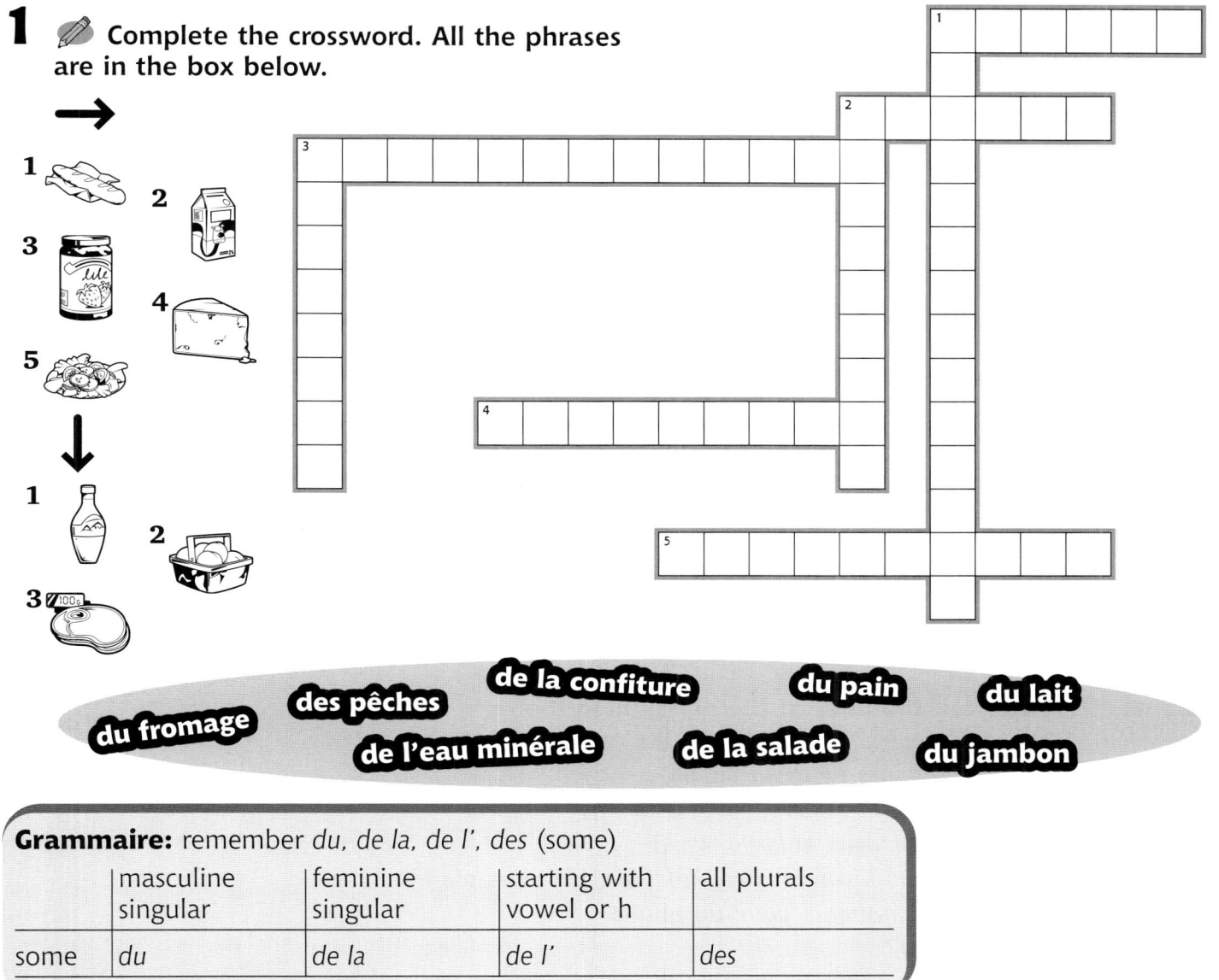

1
2
3
4
5

1
2
3

du fromage   des pêches   de la confiture   du pain   du lait

de l'eau minérale   de la salade   du jambon

Grammaire: remember *du, de la, de l', des* (some)

	masculine singular	feminine singular	starting with vowel or h	all plurals
some	*du*	*de la*	*de l'*	*des*

2 🖊 Choose the correct word for 'some' to complete the sentences.

Le matin normalement, je prends **du/de la/des** pain (*m*) avec **du/de la/des** beurre (*m*) et **du/de la/des** confiture (*f*).

Je bois **du/de la/des** thé (*m*) avec **du/de la/des** sucre (*m*).

Au collège, je mange **du/de la/des** biscuits (*mpl*) ou **du/de la/des** chips (*fpl*).

À midi, je prends **du/de la/des** pain (*m*) avec **du/de la/des** fromage (*m*) ou **du/de la/des** salade (*f*).

Je bois **du/de l'/de la** eau minérale (*f*).

⚠ ● You can see from (*f*) and (*m*) which words are masculine or feminine and which are plural (*pl*).
● Be careful! One of the words starts with a vowel so will need *de l'*.

● ask for tickets at a museum

1 How many numbers can you find in the wordsnake? Write out the words and then write them out in figures.

vingt-neuf = 29

_____

_____

_____

_____

_____

_____   _____

_____   _____

_____   _____

quarante-huitcinquante-sixcinquante- ... neufsoixante-deuxsoixante-seizequatre-vingtsquatre-vingt-troisquatre-vingt-dix-huit-vingt-quatredeuxquarante-troisquarante-trentetrentevingt-neuf

2 a Write out the lines of the dialogue in the right order.

– Trois euros cinquante pour un enfant.
– Merci, monsieur. Au revoir.
– Alors, un adulte et deux enfants. Voilà.
– Bonjour, monsieur. L'entrée, c'est combien, s'il vous plaît?
– C'est sept euros cinquante pour un adulte.
– Et pour un enfant?

_____

_____

_____

_____

_____

_____

2 b Read the dialogue with a partner. Listen to the CD to check.

Voilà! 2 Clair Workbook © Nelson Thornes 2005 Photocopying prohibited.

● read about events in French history

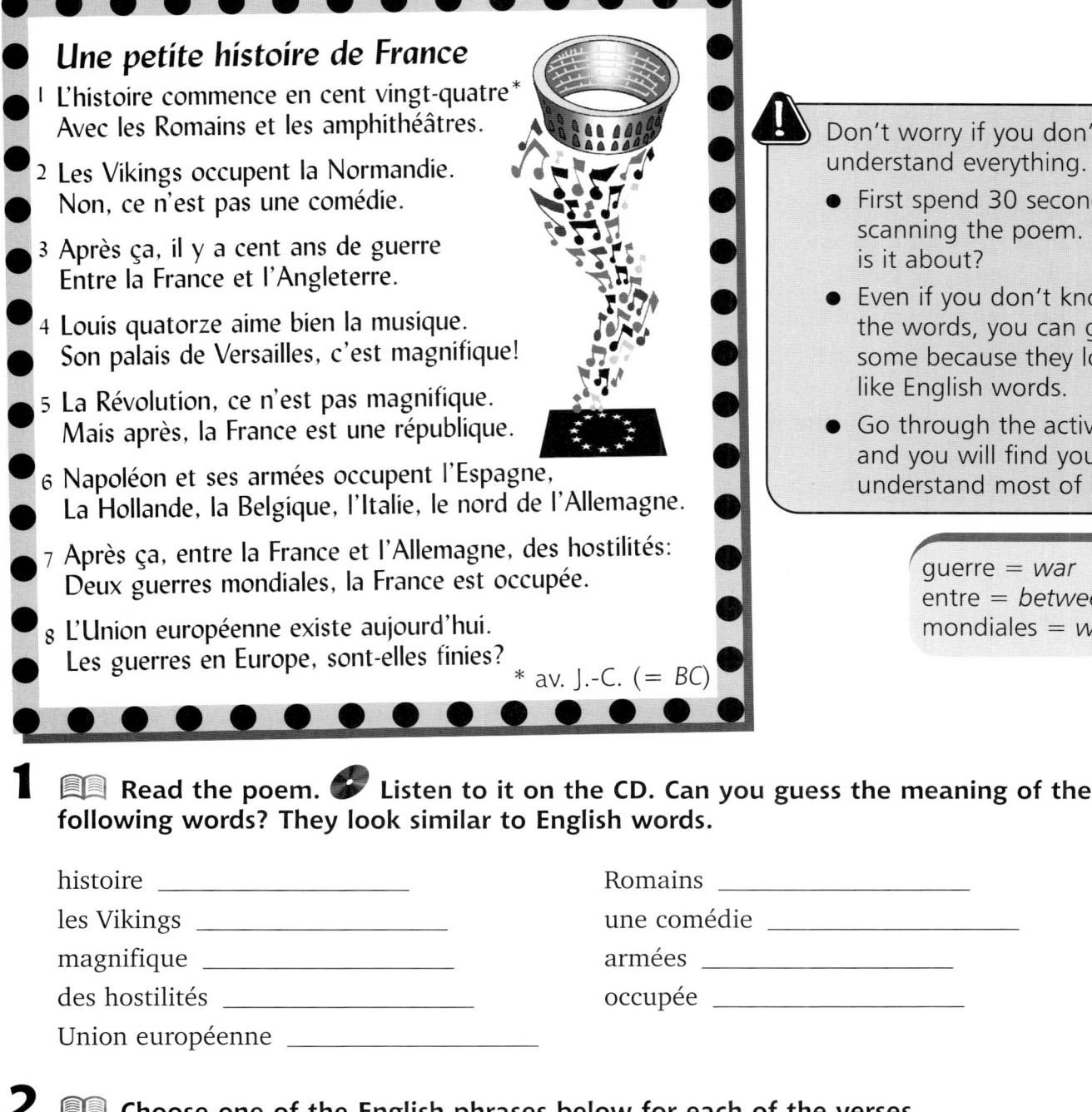

Une petite histoire de France

1 L'histoire commence en cent vingt-quatre*
Avec les Romains et les amphithéâtres.

2 Les Vikings occupent la Normandie.
Non, ce n'est pas une comédie.

3 Après ça, il y a cent ans de guerre
Entre la France et l'Angleterre.

4 Louis quatorze aime bien la musique.
Son palais de Versailles, c'est magnifique!

5 La Révolution, ce n'est pas magnifique.
Mais après, la France est une république.

6 Napoléon et ses armées occupent l'Espagne,
La Hollande, la Belgique, l'Italie, le nord de l'Allemagne.

7 Après ça, entre la France et l'Allemagne, des hostilités:
Deux guerres mondiales, la France est occupée.

8 L'Union européenne existe aujourd'hui.
Les guerres en Europe, sont-elles finies?

* av. J.-C. (= BC)

Don't worry if you don't understand everything.

● First spend 30 seconds scanning the poem. What is it about?

● Even if you don't know all the words, you can guess some because they look like English words.

● Go through the activities and you will find you can understand most of it.

guerre = *war*
entre = *between*
mondiales = *world*

1 📖 **Read the poem.** 💿 **Listen to it on the CD. Can you guess the meaning of the following words? They look similar to English words.**

histoire _____   Romains _____

les Vikings _____   une comédie _____

magnifique _____   armées _____

des hostilités _____   occupée _____

Union européenne _____

2 📖 **Choose one of the English phrases below for each of the verses.**

a After that, hostilities between France and Germany. ☐

b The European Union exists today. ☐

c Between France and England. ☐

d Napoleon and his armies occupy Spain. ☐

e With the Romans and the amphitheatres. ☐

f Louis 14th really liked music. ☐

g The revolution was not magnificent. ☐

h The Vikings occupied Normandy. ☐

cinquante-cinq **55**

● read an e-mail ● say what someone else did

> **Grammaire:** remember that to say what 'he' or 'she' did in the past, use *il a* or *elle a* + *visité, acheté,* etc.
>
> *il a mangé* – he ate
> *elle a acheté* – she bought

1 a ✎ **The English sentences should match the French ones. Find and correct the mistake in each English sentence.**

1 Il a mangé une pizza.   ⟶   **a** He is eating a pizza. _____

2 Elle a visité un musée.   ⟶   **b** He visited a museum. _____

3 Il a acheté une vidéo.   ⟶   **c** He rented a video. _____

4 Elle a fait un pique-nique.   ⟶   **d** She had lunch. _____

5 Il a visité la cathédrale.   ⟶   **e** He went in a museum. _____

1 b 📖 **Now translate the next five sentences into English.**

6 Elle a regardé la télé. _____

7 Il a acheté un T-shirt. _____

8 Elle a visité un parc safari. _____

9 Elle a fait du vélo. _____

10 Il a mangé un sandwich. _____

2 a 📖 **Read the following note and answer the questions in English.**

> Hier, mon frère a fait une excursion. Il a visité un parc safari et il a vu beaucoup d'animaux: des girafes, des éléphants, des zèbres, des hippopotames. C'était super!
> Il a acheté un T-shirt.
> À midi, il a fait un pique-nique.
> Le soir, il a joué au foot dans le parc et puis il a regardé un match de foot à la télé.
> Amitiés
> Justine

1 Where did Justine's brother go yesterday? _____

2 Name three things he saw. _____ _____ _____

3 What did he buy? _____

4 What did he do at midday? _____

5 What two things did he do in the evening? _____ _____

2 b 📖 **extra!** Now <u>underline</u> all the verbs in the past tense.

● Say all the words and expressions out loud, with a good French accent. ● Then cover the French and try to say them again. Highlight those you can't remember first time and come back to them later.

Un pique-nique *A picnic*

● *suggest what food to buy and say what you eat* ☐

on prend… _____

   du pain? _____

   du lait? _____

   du fromage? _____

   du jambon? _____

   de la confiture? _____

   de la salade? _____

   de l'eau minérale? _____

   des pêches? _____

le matin _____

au collège _____

à midi _____

je mange (parfois) _____

ou _____

Au musée (1) *At the museum (1)*

● *ask for tickets at a museum* ☐

bonjour _____

l'entrée, c'est combien, s'il vous plaît? _____

c'est *six* euros *vingt* _____

pour un adulte _____

pour un enfant _____

alors, un(e) adulte et un(e) enfant _____

voilà _____

merci _____

au revoir _____

Au musée (2) *At the museum (2)*

bonjour, monsieur _____

bonjour, madame _____

le musée ferme à quelle heure? _____

à *quinze* heures *dix* _____

merci _____

de rien _____

Un e-mail d'Ali *An email from Ali*

● *say what someone else did* ☐

hier _____

à midi _____

le soir _____

il a visité le musée _____

il a acheté une vidéo _____

elle a regardé la vidéo _____

elle a fait un pique-nique _____

cross-topic words

c'est combien? ____ s'il vous plaît ____

_____

_____

Voilà! 2 Clair Workbook © Nelson Thornes 2005

● say which presents you like ● say why you like or dislike them

1 📖 Circle the correct word for 'this' or 'these' each time.

Grammaire: remember how to say 'this' or 'these'

masculine nouns	feminine nouns	all plural nouns
ce *livre*	**cette** *trousse*	**ces** *gants*
this book	this pencil case	these gloves

1  ce/cette/ces T-shirt (*m*)

2  ce/cette/ces CD (*m*)

3  ce/cette/ces pizza (*f*)

4  ce/cette/ces vidéo (*f*)

5 ce/cette/ces cartes postales (*fpl*)

2 ✏️ Prepare a questionnaire for your friends. Write out a question for each picture.

Questionnaire: les cadeaux

Tu aimes... ? **Exemple:** *Tu aimes ces gants?*

_____ ☐ ☐

_____ ☐ ☐

_____ ☐ ☐

_____ ☐ ☐

_____ ☐ ☐

_____ ☐ ☐

ces gants	cette gourde
ce réveil	ce livre
cette trousse	
ces boucles d'oreille	

3 💬 **extra!** Ask your partner the questions you've written in exercise 2. Then give your answers to your partner.

Exemple:

A Tu aimes ces gants?

B Oui, j'aime bien. C'est un cadeau original.

Oui, j'aime bien.
Non, je n'aime pas.
C'est un cadeau...
   amusant.
   original.
   barbant.

● exchange contact details ● say phone numbers

1 📖 Complete the following phone numbers in figures.

1	zéro trois, trente-six, cinquante-huit, seize, zéro huit	03 ___ 5_ 16 0_
2	zéro deux, vingt-sept, quatre-vingts, soixante-deux, douze	___ 2_ 80 6_ ___
3	zéro neuf, soixante-treize, quatre-vingt-trois, onze, dix-neuf	0_ 73 8_ ___ 1_
4	zéro quatre, quinze, quarante-neuf, trente-huit, treize	___ ___ _9 _8 13
5	zéro six, dix-huit, soixante-quatre, quatorze, dix-sept	0_ 18 _4 14 ___
6	zéro cinq, dix, vingt, soixante, vingt-trois	___ 10 ___ _0 2_
7	zéro trois, trente-cinq, quarante-deux, soixante-trois, cinquante	_3 _5 _2 _3 5_
8	zéro quatre, dix-huit, cinquante-deux, vingt-neuf, douze	0_ 1_ 5_ 2_ 1_

2 🗩 Say the numbers in exercise 1 out loud with a partner. How quickly can your partner work out which one you're saying?

3 ✏️ Copy out the questions in the right place in the conversation.

_____

– Mon adresse, c'est 11, rue Farouk.

_____

– F-A-R-O-U-K.

_____

– C'est 16100 Cognac.

_____

– Mon numéro de téléphone, c'est le 05-46-56-82-12.

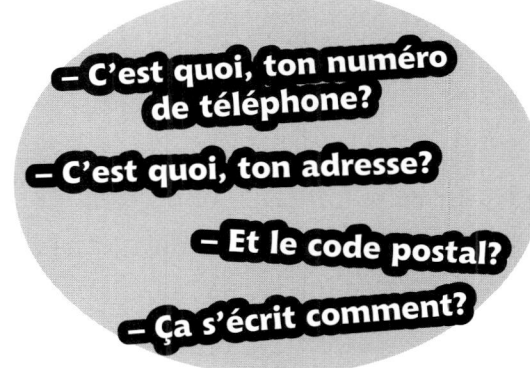

– C'est quoi, ton numéro de téléphone?

– C'est quoi, ton adresse?

– Et le code postal?

– Ça s'écrit comment?

4 a 🎤🗩 Read out the conversation in exercise 3 with a partner. Be careful with your pronunciation.

💿 Listen to the CD to check.

4 b 🗩 *extra!* In the conversation, can you give other answers to the questions? They can be your own answers or you can invent them.

cinquante-neuf   59

● recycle language from earlier units ● answer in longer sentences

1 ✎ Write out the right question from the list for each answer.

- Samedi, je vais aller au cinéma et dimanche, je vais aller chez mon père.

- Samedi dernier, j'ai joué au football et j'ai joué au basket. C'était génial!

- Le week-end, on mange ensemble et on va au centre commercial.

- J'habite à Malton. Il y a une gare et un supermarché, mais il n'y a pas de centre sportif.

- Oui, j'aime ça, mais je n'aime pas le poisson.

- Hier, après le collège, j'ai fait mes devoirs. C'était barbant!

- Ma star préférée, c'est Thierry Henri. Il est footballeur. Il est français, riche et très beau!

- Non, je ne peux pas parce que je dois aller chez mes grands-parents.

1 Qu'est-ce que tu as fait samedi dernier? (*Unit 2*)
2 Tu aimes la cuisine indienne? (*Unit 3*)
3 Tu habites où? (*Unit 4*)
4 C'est qui, ta star préférée? (*Unit 5*)
5 Vous faites quoi le week-end? (*Unit 6*)
6 Tu veux faire du vélo? (*Unit 7*)
7 Qu'est-ce que tu as fait hier? (*Unit 8*)
8 Qu'est-ce que tu vas faire ce week-end? (*Unit 9*)

2 🎤 Read the interview with a partner. Be careful with your pronunciation.
💿 Listen to the CD to check.

3 ✎ Now try writing your own answers to the questions in exercise 1. Use the space at the bottom of page 61.

⚠️
- You can adapt the answers above if you wish; just change one or two words.
- If you want to use different vocabulary, look at the *Sommaire* page for the units mentioned.
- Remember ways of making sentences longer:
  – link sentences with *et* (and), *mais* (but).
  – give your opinion: *c'est amusant, c'est barbant*, etc.

soixante

- Use your own method to help you learn the vocabulary below.
- Look back at the other *Sommaire* pages to remind yourself of different ways of learning vocabulary.

- Go back to see what you can remember from earlier units. Choose a unit you did earlier in the year and test yourself on the vocabulary.

- Don't worry if you don't remember everything, but you should find that you can remember a lot of the language you have covered.

Préparations *Preparations*

- *say which presents you like and why* ☐

tu aimes… ? _____

j'aime… _____

je n'aime pas… _____

   ce livre _____

   ce réveil _____

   cette trousse _____

   cette gourde _____

   ces gants _____

   ces boucles
   d'oreilles _____

oui, j'aime bien _____

pourquoi? _____

c'est un cadeau
  amusant _____

c'est un cadeau
  original _____

c'est un cadeau
  barbant _____

La soirée de Marine *Marine's party*

- *exchange contact details* ☐

c'est quoi, ton
  adresse? _____

mon adresse, c'est… _____

ça s'écrit comment? _____

c'est quoi, le code
  postal? _____

c'est quoi, ton numéro
  de téléphone? _____

mon numéro, c'est
  le zéro un, … _____

- Make a note below of the ways you find best to help you learn and remember your vocabulary.

_____
_____
_____
_____
_____

_____
_____
_____
_____
_____
_____
_____
_____

Cross-topic words un peu _____ c'est _____

Voilà! 2 Clair Workbook © Nelson Thornes 2005

Voilà! 2 components

Student's Book	978 0 7487 9094 4
Student's Book Clair	978 0 7487 9090 6
Teacher's Book	978 0 7487 9095 1
Teacher's Book Clair	978 0 7487 9091 3
Resource and Assessment File	978 0 7487 9098 2
Workbook (pack of 5)	978 0 7487 9097 5
Workbook Clair (pack of 5)	978 0 7487 9093 7
Audio CD Pack	978 0 7487 9096 8
Audio CD Pack Clair	978 0 7487 9092 0
Flashcards and OHTs CD-Rom	978 0 7487 9099 9
ICT Resource (*Just Click*)	978 0 7487 9382 2

Nelson Thornes

a Wolters Kluwer business

ISBN 978-0-7487-9606-9

9 780748 796069